BY THE SAME AUTHOR:

American Education: The Metropolitan Experience, 1876–1980
American Education: The National Experience, 1783–1876
American Education: The Colonial Experience, 1607–1783
Traditions of American Education
Public Education
The Genius of American Education
The Wonderful World of Ellwood Patterson Cubberley
The Transformation of the School
The American Common School

POPULAR EDUCATION
AND ITS DISCONTENTS

POPULAR EDUCATION

AND

ITS DISCONTENTS

Lawrence A. Cremin

1817

HARPER & ROW, PUBLISHERS, New York
Grand Rapids, Philadelphia, St. Louis, San Francisco
London, Singapore, Sydney, Tokyo, Toronto

The Inglis and Burton Lectures
Harvard Graduate School of Education
March 1989

POPULAR EDUCATION AND ITS DISCONTENTS. Copyright © 1990 by
Lawrence A. Cremin. All rights reserved. Printed in the United
States of America. No part of this book may be used or reproduced
in any manner whatsoever without written permission except in the
case of brief quotations embodied in critical articles and reviews.
For information address Harper & Row, Publishers, Inc., 10 E. 53rd
Street, New York, N.Y. 10022.

FIRST EDITION

Designer: Barbara DuPree Knowles

LIBRARY OF CONGRESS CATALOGING-IN-PUBLICATION DATA

Cremin, Lawrence Arthur, 1925–
    Popular education and its discontents/Lawrence A. Cremin.
        p. cm.
    "The Inglis and Burton lectures, Harvard Graduate School of
Education, March 1989."
    Includes index.
    ISBN 0-06-016270-8
        1. Education and state—United States. 2. Education—Philoso-
phy.
3. Educational sociology—United States. 4. Education—United
States—History—20th century. I. Title. II. Title: Inglis and
Burton lectures.
LC89.C7 1989
370'.1—dc20   89-45644

90 91 92 93 94 CC/RRD 10 9 8 7 6 5 4 3 2 1

CONTENTS

PREFACE   *vii*

Popular Schooling   *1*

The Cacophony of Teaching   *51*

Education as Politics   *85*

INDEX   *129*

PREFACE

I was deeply grateful in the autumn of 1987 for the invitation from Dean Patricia Albjerg Graham and her colleagues to give the Inglis and Burton Lectures at the Harvard Graduate School of Education. I had recently completed *American Education: The Metropolitan Experience, 1876–1980,* the final volume of my trilogy on the history of American education; and, beyond the high honor implicit in the invitation, it occurred to me that the lectures would provide a very special opportunity to reflect upon certain present-day problems of American education in the context of American educational traditions. The lectures were delivered on March 2, 9, and 16, 1989, and the present volume sets forth their substance in expanded form. It stands, in a sense, as a coda to the trilogy.

I ended *American Education: The Metropolitan Experience* with the argument that there had been three abiding characteristics of American education—first, *popularization,* the tendency to make education widely available in forms that are increasingly accessible to diverse peoples; second, *multitudinousness,* the proliferation and multiplication of institutions to provide that wide availability and that increasing accessibility; and third, *politicization,* the effort to solve certain social problems indirectly through education instead of directly through politics. None of these characteristics has been uniquely American—we can see them at work in any number of other countries—and yet the three in tandem have marked American education uniquely. As I argued in the final volume of the trilogy, they have been associated with some of the formidable achievements of American education at the same time that they have created some of its most intractable problems. It is this combination of achievements and problems and its bearing on present-day educational policy that I explore in the essays that follow.

The first essay deals with the rising chorus of dissatisfaction, especially with regard to academic standards, that has accompanied the popularization of education in the United States since the middle of the nineteenth century. My argument there is that the ideal of popular schooling is as radical an ideal as Americans have embraced; that we have made great progress in moving toward the ideal, however imperfect the institutions we have established to achieve it; and that it is essential for our kind of society to continue the effort. I argue further, however, that our recent assessments of how far we have come, especially as those assessments have been expressed in the policy literature of the 1980s, have been seriously flawed by a failure to understand the extraordinary complexity of education—a failure to grasp the impossibility of defining a good school apart from its social and intellectual context, the impossibility of even comprehending the processes and effects of schooling and, in fact, its successes and failures apart from their embedment in a larger ecology of education that includes what families, television broadcasters, workplaces, and a host of other institutions are contributing at any given time.

The second essay explores the radical changes that have occurred in those nonschool institutions of education since World War II, especially in the education provided by families and workplaces as well as the education (and miseducation) provided by television. My argument there is that we need to recognize that schools and colleges cannot accomplish the educational tasks of a modern postindustrial civilization on their own, that a broader approach to education is demanded, one that considers schools and colleges as crucially important but not solely responsible for teaching and learning. And I point to some of the issues that seem to me inescapably involved in the crafting of a more comprehensive set of educational policies for our time.

The third essay examines the longstanding tendency of Americans to try to solve certain social problems indirectly through education rather than directly through politics. My argument there is that this phenomenon places enormous burdens on the schools and colleges, of millennial hopes and expectations, at the same time that it involves education in the most fundamental aspirations of the society. I argue further that the phenomenon by its very nature calls for a much more extensive body of tested knowledge about the institutions and processes of education than is now available to those charged with the development of educational policy and the conduct of educational practice. In the absence of such knowledge, I believe it is folly to talk about excellence in American education.

I should like to express my appreciation to Patricia Albjerg Graham and Loren R. Graham for their gracious encouragement and warm hospitality during my several visits to Harvard in March 1989. In addition, I owe a special debt of gratitude to my colleague Ellen Condliffe Lagemann. She and I have co-taught courses in the history of American education and contemporary educational policy during the past ten years, from which much of the substance of *Popular Education and Its Discontents* has been drawn; and in any number of instances in the development of the material it was quite impossible to determine where my ideas ended and hers began. She was also kind enough to read and comment upon successive drafts of the manuscript. The book has surely benefited from her wisdom, though responsibility for its shortcomings is solely mine. Sarah Henry Lederman assisted me throughout with the research, and Alissa Beth Burstein typed more versions of the manuscript than she would care to remember. Finally, I should like to acknowledge the generous support of the Carnegie Corporation of New York for my research and writing over the past quarter century. No scholar has ever had more patient or steadfast encouragement.

L.A.C.

POPULAR
SCHOOLING

Every nation, and therefore every national system of education, has the defects of its qualities.   —SIR MICHAEL SADLER,
"Impressions of American Education"

I

The popularization of American schools and colleges
since the end of World War II has been nothing short of
phenomenal, involving an unprecedented broadening of
access, an unprecedented diversification of curricula, and
an unprecedented extension of public control. In 1950, 34
percent of the American population twenty-five years of age
or older had completed at least four years of high school,
while 6 percent of that population had completed at least
four years of college. By 1985, 74 percent of the American
population twenty-five years of age or older had completed
at least four years of high school, while 19 percent had
completed at least four years of college. During that same
thirty-five year period, school and college curricula broadened and diversified tremendously, in part because of the
existential fact of more diverse student bodies with more
diverse needs, interests, abilities, and styles of learning; in
part because of the accelerating growth of knowledge and
new fields of knowledge; in part because of the rapid development of the American economy and its demands on

school systems; and in part because of the transformation of America's role in the world. The traditional subjects could be studied in a greater range of forms; the entry of new subjects into curricula provided a greater range of choice; and the effort to combine subjects into new versions of general education created a greater range of requirements. Finally, the rapid increase in the amount of state and federal funds invested in the schools and colleges, coupled with the rising demand for access on the part of segments of the population traditionally held at the margins, brought a corresponding development of the instruments of public oversight and control—local community boards, state coordinating boards, court-appointed masters and monitors, and federal attorneys with the authority to enforce federal regulations. In the process, American schools became at the same time both more centralized and more decentralized.[1]

It was in many ways a remarkable achievement, of which Americans could be justifiably proud. Yet it seemed to bring with it a pervasive sense of failure. During the 1970s, there was widespread suspicion that American students were falling behind in international competition, that while more people were going to school for ever longer periods of time, they were learning less and less. And in the 1980s, that suspicion seemed to be confirmed by the strident rhetoric of the National Commission on Excellence in Education. Recall the commission's charges in *A Nation at Risk:*

> We report to the American people that while we can take justifiable pride in what our schools and colleges have historically accomplished and contributed to the United States and the well-being of its people, the educational foundations of our society are presently being eroded by a rising tide of mediocrity that threatens our very future as a Nation and a people. What was unimaginable a genera-

tion ago has begun to happen—others are matching and surpassing our educational attainments.

   If an unfriendly power had attempted to impose on America the mediocre educational performance that exists today, we might well have viewed it as an act of war. As it stands, we have allowed this to happen to ourselves.[2]

Now, there have always been critics of the schools and colleges. From the very beginning of the public school crusade in the nineteenth century, there were those who thought that popular schooling was at best a foolish idea and at worst a subversive idea. The editor of the Philadelphia *National Gazette* argued in the 1830s that free universal education was nothing more than a harebrained scheme of social radicals, and claimed that it was absolutely illegal and immoral to tax one part of the community to educate the children of another. And beyond such wholesale opposition, even those who favored the idea of universal education thought that the results were unimpressive. The educator Frederick Packard lamented that the schools were failing dismally in even their most fundamental tasks. He charged on the basis of personal visits to classrooms that nine out of ten youngsters were unable to read a newspaper, keep a simple debit and credit account, or draft an ordinary business letter. The writer James Fenimore Cooper was ready to grant that the lower schools were developing a greater range of talent than was the case in most other countries, but he pointed to what he thought was the superficiality of much of the work of the colleges and bemoaned the absence of genuine accomplishment in literature and the arts. And the French commentator Alexis de Tocqueville, echoing the English critic Sydney Smith, observed that America had produced few writers of distinction, no great artists, and not a single first-class poet. Americans were a practical people, he concluded, but not very speculative. They could boast many lawyers but no jurists, many good workers but few imaginative inventors.[3]

By the early years of the twentieth century, as some elementary education was becoming nearly universal and as secondary education was beginning to be popularized, the criticism became broader and sharper. A writer in *Gunton's Magazine* charged that as schooling had spread it had been made too easy and too entertaining. "The mental nourishment we spoonfeed our children," he observed, "is not only minced but peptonized so that their brains digest it without effort and without benefit and the result is the anaemic intelligence of the average American schoolchild." And a Maryland farmer named Francis Livesey became so outraged at the whole idea of free universal education that he organized a society called the Herbert Spencer Education Club with two classes of membership—one for those seeking the complete abolition of public schooling and one for those willing to settle for the repeal of all compulsory attendance laws.[4]

With respect to secondary and higher education, critics such as Irving Babbitt, Abraham Flexner, and Robert Hutchins leveled blast after blast against the relaxation of language requirements, the overcrowding of curricula with narrow technical courses, and the willingness to permit students to work out their own programs of study. The spread of educational opportunity in the United States, they observed, reflected less a spirit of democratic fairness than a willingness to prolong adolescence. The result was an inferior educational product at every level—high school programs were too watered down and fragmented; the colleges were graduating men and women unable to write and spell a decent English and pitifully ignorant of mathematics, the sciences, and modern languages; and the graduate schools were crowded with students of mediocre ability who lacked the slightest appreciation of higher culture.[5]

Even those foreign observers who were prone to admire the American commitment to popular schooling wrung their hands at what they saw as the widespread absence of high intellectual expectations, particularly at the high school and college levels. Thus, Sir Michael Sadler, the director of the Office of Special Inquiries and Reports of the British government, and a great friend of the United States, noted an absence of intellectual discipline and rigor in American schools—too much candy and ice cream, he liked to say, and not enough oatmeal porridge. And Erich Hylla, a member of the German ministry of education who had spent a year in residence at Teachers College, Columbia University, and who translated Dewey's *Democracy and Education* into German, lamented what he perceived as the disjointedness and superficiality of secondary and undergraduate study and the resultant poor achievement of American students.[6]

As popularization advanced at every level of schooling after World War II, the drumbeat of dissatisfaction grew louder. Arthur Bestor and Hyman Rickover argued during the 1950s and 1960s that popular schooling had been literally subverted by an interlocking directorate of education professors, state education officials, and professional association leaders; they charged that the basics had been ignored in favor of a trivial curriculum parading under the name of Life Adjustment Education and that as a result American freedom was in jeopardy. Robert Hutchins continued his mordant criticisms of the 1930s, contending that the so-called higher learning purveyed by the colleges and universities was neither higher nor learning but rather a collection of trade school courses intended to help young people win the material success that Americans prized so highly. And again, even those foreign observers who were disposed to admire the American commitment to popular education now made it something of a litany to comment on what they perceived to be the low standards and mediocre achievements of American students. The English political economist Harold Laski noted the readiness of American parents to expect too little of their youngsters and the readiness of the youngsters to see interest in abstract ideas as somewhat strange at best, with the result that American college graduates seemed to him to be two to three years less intellectually mature than their English or French counterparts. And the Scottish political scientist D. W. Brogan was quite prepared to grant that the American public school had been busy Americanizing immigrants for several generations at least—he liked to refer to the public school as "the formally unestablished national church of the United States"—but he saw the price of that emphasis on social goals as an insufficient attention to intellectual goals. For all their talk of preparing the young for life, Brogan maintained, Americans were not being realistic about what life would actually demand during the second half of the twentieth century.[7]

Within such a context, Paul Copperman's allegations of the late 1970s that Americans of that generation would be the first whose educational skills would not surpass or equal or even approach those of their parents, which the National Commission on Excellence in Education quoted approvingly in *A Nation at Risk,* and Allan Bloom's assertions of the late 1980s that higher education had failed democracy and impoverished the souls of American students were scarcely surprising or even original. Why all the fuss, then? How, if at all, did the criticisms of the 1980s differ from those that had come before? I believe they differed in three important ways: they were more vigorous and pervasive; they were putatively buttressed by data from cross-national studies of educational achievement; and, coming at a time when Americans seemed to be feeling anxious about their place in the world, they gave every indication of being potentially more dangerous and destructive.[8]

II

The argument over standards is surely as old as the world itself. Just about the time Adam first whispered to Eve that they were living through an age of transition, the Serpent doubtless issued the first complaint that academic standards were beginning to decline. The charge of decline, of course, can embrace many different meanings and serve as a surrogate for a wide variety of discontents, only one of which may be that young people are actually learning less. As often as not, it suggests that young people are learning less of what a particular commentator or group of commentators believe they ought to be learning, and the "ought" derives ultimately from a conception of education and of the educated person.

One can observe this in the very different views of John Dewey and Robert Hutchins. For Dewey, education was a process of growth that had no end beyond itself, a process in which individuals were constantly extending their knowledge, informing their judgments, refining their sensibilities, and illuminating their moral choices. For Hutchins, education was nothing more or less than the cultivation of the intellect, the training of the mind, and there was a group of what he called "permanent studies" that had long been of proven value in achieving that end, namely, the arts of reading, writing, thinking, and speaking, together with mathematics, which he saw as "the best exemplar of the processes of human reason." Dewey and Hutchins had radically different conceptions of the educated person, and while both would doubtless have wanted young people to read, write, speak, and think effectively, they would—and indeed they did—have profoundly different standards by which they judged academic achievement.[9]

Hutchins's idea of permanent studies offers an important clue to some of the principal differences that marked their longstanding disagreements over education. Hutchins lamented the "disunity, discord, and disorder" that characterized the world of learning, the emphasis on narrow practicality, on scientific empiricism, and on a false notion of democracy that assumed everyone had a right to a higher education. And, by way of a remedy, he proposed study of the great classics of the West—the works of Plato, Aristotle, Augustine, Spinoza, and Shakespeare—along with the fundamental problems of the social sciences, the natural sciences, and, above all, metaphysics. He saw these as enduring subjects that would remove education from the flux of the present and endow it with the timelessness he believed must mark any education of worth.

Dewey also lamented the conflict and confusion that characterized the world of learning, but he sought solutions not in what he saw as a retreat into traditionalism but rather in a radical reconstruction of liberal education that would unite it with vocational and professional education and render it burningly relevant to the flux of the present. He thought that vocationalism and practicality were exerting their demands on the schools and colleges precisely because the arts and techniques of a modern economy had rendered older methods of apprenticeship beside the point. And he saw new knowledge being generated in such abundance that the old walls between subjects were rapidly breaking down, and wholly new fields such as astrophysics, biochemistry, and physiological psychology were coming into being. Further, he saw the substance of the subjects themselves being radically transformed as new problematics took the place of older formulations—the quantum description of physical phenomena replacing the classical description, the stuff of social and intellectual history replacing the traditional account of wars and rebellions, the newer criticism replacing the older study of literature in its cultural context. For Dewey, Hutchins's enthronement of metaphysics would render education irrelevant at best, authoritarian at worst; for Hutchins, Dewey's effort to incorporate the vocational would render education ephemeral at best, trivial at worst. The standards by which each might judge an education worthy were utterly incompatible.

To draw the differences between a Dewey and a Hutchins is to maintain the argument on its own academic terms. But standards involve much more than determinations of what knowledge is of most worth; they also involve social and cultural differences, and they frequently serve as symbols and surrogates for those differences. People who disagree with the religious orientation of a school or college will commonly charge it with low standards—this phenomenon was at the heart of the attack by Christian fundamentalists on the public schools of Charleston, West Virginia, during the early 1970s. People who have social aspirations will often seek admission for their children to independent schools, which they perceive as having high standards, in place of public schools, which they perceive as having low standards. People who wish to avoid racially mixed schools will occasionally place their children in predominantly white private schools, which they perceive as having high standards, instead of racially integrated public schools, which they perceive as having low standards. In such cases, the perceptions may or may not conform to reality. But as

James S. Coleman and Thomas Hoffer have argued, the very choices on the part of parents may create a measure of mutual support between home and school and thereby contribute to the formation of a like-minded community of parents surrounding the school that intensifies the education of the students and makes a self-fulfilling prophecy of the choice.[10]

To note the inseparability of academic standards and value orientations is also to call to mind the discontent felt by those who perceive themselves as outside the system, so to speak, and are therefore resistant to any kind of schooling sponsored by the so-called establishment. The anthropologist John U. Ogbu has documented this phenomenon among certain African-American subcommunities who see themselves as oppressed by the dominant white society and who perceive the schools maintained by that society as instruments for socializing their children to subservient roles. For the children to do well in school, Ogbu argues, is to "buy into oppression"; given the reality of compulsory attendance, their only option other than truancy is to fail. In essence, Ogbu is contending that the children's failure is a rejection of the standards and values of the establishment. Ogbu distinguishes sharply between the situation of native-born African-Americans and of recently arrived immigrants. In my own view, similar phenomena of alienation can be observed among working-class families in some communities and ethnoreligious minority families in others. They too develop what anthropologists have called "cultures of resistance." They too reject the standards and values of what they perceive as the dominant society.[11]

There is a kindred point to be made about academic standards serving as surrogates for social criticisms or aspirations, namely, that social groups possessing a relatively rare and highly valued commodity that establishes their superiority over other social groups are reluctant to see that commodity more widely distributed. Wide distribution becomes tantamount to devaluation, and there is a sense of what Alvin Toffler has called violated exclusivity on the part of those who have held the commodity. As more people come into the possession of the commodity, it seems easier to obtain, and, in fact, if alternative routes are created to obtain the commodity, those routes become in the minds of those whose exclusivity has been violated lesser routes marked by lower standards. The violation is often felt most keenly by those who have attained the commodity most recently; having achieved the goal, they find it less of an achievement since too many others are achieving it at the same time.[12]

Beyond the problem of violated exclusivity, there is the phenomenon of bequeathed aspirations—the setting of standards for the young that the adults setting the standards have been unable or unwilling to meet themselves. A beautifully ironic example occurred at a press conference called by the National Geographic Society during the summer of 1988 to announce the results of an international survey the society had commissioned to determine how many adults could find thirteen selected countries, Central America, the Pacific Ocean, and the Persian Gulf on an unmarked world map. The American results were dismal. "Have you heard of the lost generation?" Gilbert M. Grosvenor, president of the society, observed sarcastically of his countrymen at the press conference. "We have found them. They are lost. They haven't the faintest idea of where they are." To remedy the situation, the society announced plans for a major curriculum development effort in the field of geography. Meanwhile, when one of the reporters at the press conference asked Grosvenor whether he could identify the states contiguous with Texas, Grosvenor found himself unable to do so! We should not be surprised when the young are occasionally skeptical of the standards laid upon them.[13]

III

Adults express their discontents with popular education through the pen, the ballot box, and the checkbook; the young most often vote with their feet—they leave. In recent decades we have referred to leaving as "dropping out," though the very phrase puts a construction on the process that is itself time-bound: it assumes the youngsters really belong in school. Throughout most of the history of popular education in the United States, people assumed that children would obtain as much schooling as they and their parents deemed appropriate or financially feasible, and they would then go off to work, or, in the case of young women, begin the business of homemaking or childrearing. By 1940, the average American adult had completed 8.6 years of schooling, while younger adults between the ages of twenty-five and twenty-nine had completed 10.3 years of schooling. Clearly, the normal expectation for the average American child on the eve of World War II was the completion of elementary schooling and the continuation on to some secondary schooling, with only about half the seventeen- and eighteen-year-olds completing secondary schooling (these averages, incidentally, should not mask the considerable differences between males and females, blacks and whites, Hispanics and Anglos, northerners and southerners, urbanites and rural people, and well-to-do people and poor people).[14]

We have a fairly good idea of the reasons youngsters left school during this period. Other than problems with their own health or the health of family members, the most common reason cited was the decision to go to work. As early as 1909, however, when Leonard Ayres published the first systematic study of retardation and elimination (expulsion or dropping out) in city school systems, reasons such as academic failure, lack of ability, or dissatisfaction with schooling itself—reasons that Ayres combined under the rubric "lack of success"—were seen as significant. Ayres himself concluded that lack of success in school was the greatest single cause that impelled pupils to drop out. Further, he argued that for youngsters to drop out before graduation from elementary school was prima facie evidence of inefficiency in the school system, an inefficiency that was costly to society and to those who dropped out. Since Ayres believed that the mission of the common school was to give the largest possible proportion of the children of the community a complete elementary schooling, he saw the need for a fundamental reform of the course of study that would offer all children the same sense of success that bright children were experiencing during their schooling and would offer boys the same sense of success that girls were enjoying.[15]

Over the next thirty years Americans came to make the same assumptions about secondary education. George Counts concluded his pioneering study of the selective character of American secondary education in 1922 with the finding that secondary education had not been "education for adolescence," as elementary education was "education for childhood," but remained instead education for a select group of adolescents who were privileged by way of race, class, and ethnicity. And believing as he did that democracy demanded universal education through the secondary level, he recommended the appropriate broadening of high school programs and concomitant adaptations of subject matter and methods of instruction that would make universal education through the secondary school achievable. Not only professional educators but state legislators and governors adopted the goal—by the 1920s the mean legal school leaving age was between sixteen and seventeen years, with a few states requiring attendance only until age fourteen and a few requiring attendance until age eighteen. Moreover, as school attendance laws came to be enforced in combination with child labor laws, there was widespread movement toward the goal. Educators talked enthusiastically of increasing the so-called holding power of the schools, and Ayres's conclusion that inefficiency in the school system had largely caused the high dropout rate in elementary schools was extended to the dropout rate in secondary schools.[16]

Secondary school enrollments doubled during the 1920s and then again during the 1930s. Nevertheless, the extensive studies of young people during the Depression, when youth unemployment was at an all-time high, indicated significant continuity in the reasons youngsters left school. They dropped out mostly because they could not afford to stay in; even with free tuition, the modest charges for books and assorted student activities, coupled with the loss of forgone earnings, proved prohibitive. Also, along with economic reasons, there were the reasons Ayres had grouped under "lack of success," namely, academic failure, perceived lack of ability, and dissatisfaction with the curriculum. In addition, there were the contradictions students felt between the assumption that staying in school would increase their earning power and the reality that there were simply no jobs. This contradiction would continue to beset the effort to bring the most disadvantaged segments of the population within the purview of the secondary school.

The post–World War II popularization of schooling

combined two elements: the drive to make secondary schooling universal in the United States and the drive to extend the opportunity for higher education to all who wished it and were qualified. The first was presaged in a widely read document prepared by the Educational Policies Commission of the National Education Association and the American Association of School Administrators entitled *Education for ALL American Youth* (1944). It recommended the extension of the legal age of compulsory schooling to eighteen; it outlined a vastly broadened curriculum appropriate to the heterogeneous clientele that would be entering the high schools, a curriculum that would provide vocational as well as academic instruction keyed to the interests of adolescents and the skills they would need to function effectively as parents, citizens, and workers; and it envisioned an upward extension of secondary education that would embrace local junior colleges offering vocational as well as general education.[17]

The second drive was presaged in the report of President Harry S. Truman's Commission on Higher Education entitled *Higher Education for American Democracy* (1948). It argued that American colleges and universities could no longer serve democracy by merely turning out an intellectual elite; they would also have to become "the means by which every citizen, youth, and adult is enabled and encouraged to carry his education, formal and informal, as far as his native capacities permit." It asserted that at least 49 percent of the American population had the mental ability to complete fourteen or more years of schooling and that at least 32 percent had the mental ability to complete an advanced liberal or professional education. And it recommended that a principal means of achieving this goal be the community junior college, which would offer a semiprofessional education mixing "a goodly amount of general education for personal and social development with technical education that is intensive, accurate, and comprehensive enough to give the student command of marketable abilities."[18]

Enrollments in grades nine to twelve rose steadily from 1940 to 1975, when they began to fall off as a result of the declining numbers of fourteen- to seventeen-year-olds. Enrollments in grades nine to twelve as a percentage of the population fourteen to seventeen years of age rose from 73 percent in 1940 to 93 percent in 1971 and then fluctuated between 90 percent and 94 percent thereafter. The number of high school graduates as a percentage of the seventeen-year-old population peaked in 1968–69 at 77 percent, fell off to a low of 71 percent in 1979–80, and then rose again to 74 percent in 1983–84, though if one were to add the number of those who subsequently earned a General Education Development credential, the overall percentage of high school graduates would rise to 85 or 86 percent. At the higher education level, spurred initially by veterans studying under the provisions of the Servicemen's Readjustment Act of 1944, enrollments in colleges and universities rose rapidly during the late 1940s, slipped briefly during the early 1950s, and then rose steadily after 1953 to a point where by 1968 half the population eighteen and nineteen years of age and roughly a third of the population twenty and twenty-one years of age were enrolled in postsecondary education; both statistics fluctuated thereafter, standing at 52 percent and 36 percent, respectively, in 1985. By the mid-1980s, 22 percent of young adults had completed four years of college, as compared with 11 percent in 1960 and 6 percent in 1940.[19]

As had been the case historically, these increases in enrollment were accompanied by fundamental changes in standards as those standards were embodied in school curricula. Actually, the schools in the immediate post–World

War II period were dominated by two powerful assumptions bequeathed by the progressive education movement. The first assumption was that to hold ever greater percentages of youngsters for ever longer periods of time, what was needed was a dramatic expansion in the number of programmatic options—options such as vocational courses and courses in civics, health, recreation, and personal development. The second assumption was that the substance of the traditional subjects needed to be transformed so as to make them more interesting and more teachable to the new groups of young people coming into the secondary school and that the best way of doing this was to make the subjects useful. Traditional arithmetic would have to become consumer arithmetic. Traditional science would have to become utilitarian science—the kind of physics that enabled one to repair one's household appliances, or the kind of biology that enabled one to look after one's health. Interestingly, there was never enough research on the nature and variety of pedagogical methods that might be necessary to teach academic arithmetic, physics, or biology to the newly heterogeneous clientele of the American high school. It proved infinitely easier to juggle the substance of the curriculum than to develop pedagogies for conveying the more intellectually demanding materials to most or all of the students.

Given the reality of state and local control, the transformation of curricula—and of educational standards—that went forward in light of these assumptions proceeded at different paces in different communities. It involved a continuing political process in which various lay publics, the several professions with a stake in schooling, and a variety of special-interest groups participated in a continuing redefinition of what a high school education would mean. And what we now look back on as the great modernizing and renewal of the academic curriculum during the 1950s and early 1960s, through such national projects as the Physical Sciences Study Committee, the Biological Sciences Curriculum Study, and the School Mathematics Study Group, simply involved the movement of academics from the elite universities into this political process, with the assistance of National Science Foundation and Office of Education funds. The academic scholars brought with them not only more up-to-date versions of their disciplines but also a very different primary assumption, namely, that subject matter did not have to be useful in some narrow, practical sense to engage youngsters but could be presented in such a way as to be interesting in its own right.

Obviously, many of these developments were also manifest in the colleges, especially in the community junior colleges, which were widely seen, in the fashion of the Truman Commission's recommendations, as upward extensions of public secondary education. Part high schools, part technical schools, part adult education facilities, part undergraduate colleges, and part community centers, the community junior colleges provided a mix of vocational, general, and academic education for all graduates of accredited secondary institutions who wished to attend. The list of occupations for which they prepared students expanded by leaps and bounds. Students could become animal health specialists, computer programmers, dental hygienists, dietetic technicians, funeral service practitioners, office managers, paralegals, paramedics, practical nurses, or X-ray technicians. At the same time the list of general and academic offerings they made available to their immensely diverse clientele ranged from the most formal courses in biology, English literature, and sociology to the most informal courses in popular culture, printmaking, and video production. The community colleges were intended in the report

of the Truman Commission to offer college-style academic
programs to those who planned to transfer to baccalaureate
granting institutions; terminal vocational and general education programs to those who wished to complete their
formal education with an Associate in Arts degree; and
individual vocational, semiprofessional, and general education courses to those who wished to extend their knowledge
or improve their skills. Actually, by the 1980s they enrolled
roughly a third of the students in higher education, but
fewer than 20 percent of those students would ever transfer
to four-year institutions and complete the work for the
bachelor's degree.[20]

The striking fact about the development of four-year
college curricula during this same era is the extent to which
they moved in many of the same directions. They may not
have included courses for dental hygienists and paralegals,
but they certainly did include courses in computer programming, nursing, and office management. And with the
demands of activist students for relevance in the 1960s and
of careerist students for utility in the 1970s, along with the
need for freshman occasioned by demographic and financial pressures in both decades, there were courses too in
popular culture, printmaking, and video production. For all
intents and purposes, except for a few highly select institutions—some 50 to 100, perhaps, out of the 2,000–odd four-
year institutions—admission and graduation requirements
had diversified to a point of near-meaninglessness.[21]

Even within this context of broadened and popularized
offerings, however, there was considerable discontent on
the part of many students. They continued to vote with
their feet. Dropouts from secondary schools remained sufficiently high so that a quarter of those in the fifth grade at
age eleven during the mid-1970s could not be expected to
graduate at age eighteen during the early 1980s. Among

those who did drop out, roughly half the boys and a third of the girls gave school-related reasons for leaving— reasons such as bad grades, dislike of study, perceived unfairness on the part of teachers, or perceived irrelevance of the curriculum. Michelle Fine questioned students in a comprehensive high school in New York City during the mid-1980s on why they stayed and why they left. She found the youngsters' choices both rational and considered. One young man who dropped out in his senior year after achieving a score of 1200 on his SATs spoke of wooden, unimaginative, and often erroneous teaching. Another saw no relation between the courses he was taking and his need to earn a living. One young woman believed that no one could make it in the real world without a high school diploma but that there would be few jobs waiting for people like her in that real world even with high school diplomas. And several young women who had recently given birth to children spoke of being made to feel unwelcome when their pregnancies became noticeable.[22]

Similarly, college was for many a revolving door. One revealing study during the late 1960s found that almost 25 percent of all college dropouts had been ambivalent about enrolling in the first place, indicating that initial uncertainty was at least one factor in eventual departure. And another study in the late 1960s found that lack of interest in courses and dissatisfaction with the college environment were the chief reasons for dropping out given by young men and the leading reasons other than marriage or the need to earn a living given by young women. A pair of studies carried out by the Carnegie Commission on Higher Education and the Carnegie Council on Policy Studies in Higher Education found that over 12 percent of the students queried in 1969 and over 8 percent of the students queried in 1976 reported that they were "dissatisfied" or "very dissatisfied" with the college they were attending. Vincent Tinto's careful review of the data of the 1980s indicated that of the nearly 2.8 million students who in 1986 would be entering higher education institutions for the first time over 1.6 million would leave their first institution without receiving a degree, and, of those, approximately 1.2 million would leave higher education altogether without ever completing a degree program of any kind. Moreover, while Tinto found the reasons for the departures, as always, complex, dissatisfaction with the college itself and with its programs, or, as Tinto graciously put it, incongruence, remained a prime cause.[23]

IV

David Cohen and Michael Garet once described policy not as a series of discrete decisions that add up to a manifest course of action but rather as a "grand story: a large and loose set of ideas about how society works, why it goes wrong and how it can be set right." If one looks at the dominant American policy statements regarding popular education since World War II, one can discern three grand stories, each quite different from the others, each with its own analysis of how education works, why it has gone wrong, and how it can be set right. The first grand story can be found in the writings of James B. Conant during the 1950s and early 1960s; the second can be found in a series of reports on the secondary schools and colleges published during the 1970s, notably the report of the Panel on Youth of the President's Science Advisory Committee entitled *Youth: Transition to Adulthood* and the reports of the Carnegie Commission on Higher Education; the third can be found in the reports during the 1980s of the National Commission on Excellence in Education entitled *A Nation at Risk* and of the Study Group on the State of Learning in the Humanities in Higher Education entitled *To Reclaim a Legacy*. [24]

The writings of James B. Conant were widely read and extraordinarily influential during the two decades following the end of World War II. Having retired from the presidency of Harvard in 1953, Conant spent the next four years as U. S. high commissioner and U. S. ambassador to West Germany and then devoted most of his time thereafter to studies and commentaries on American education. His earliest pronouncements on education had come, of course, in connection with his addresses and reports as president of Harvard, where he enunciated a Jeffersonian philosophy that embraced universal elementary education, comprehensive secondary education, and highly selective meritocratic higher education—the combination, he believed, would be America's best guarantee of a free and "classless" society. [25]

Nowhere did Conant sketch his educational program in its entirety more clearly than in his 1952 Page-Barbour Lectures at the University of Virginia, which appeared as *Education and Liberty* the following year. Contemplating the vast increase in the clientele of American schools and colleges that was clearly in the making in the 1950s, he advanced the following proposals: first, an adherence to the principle of a comprehensive high school with a common core of studies and differentiated programs but also with greater effort to identify gifted youngsters and offer them more rigorous training in languages, mathematics, and the natural sciences; second, a commitment to expand the number of junior colleges and "work experience programs" in junior colleges; third, a refusal to expand either the number or the size of four-year colleges coupled with a contraction in the number of four-year undergraduate programs in the universities, and a commitment to hold all four-year undergraduate programs to high standards; fourth, an expansion in the number of publicly and privately financed scholarships for able high school graduates who were "potential professional men and women"; fifth, continued experimentation with general education at every level for the specialized university scholar as well as for the future manual worker; and, finally, increasing collaboration between the colleges and universities and the secondary schools in the upgrading of secondary school programs. Conant added to these recommendations in several of the subsequent studies he carried out under the auspices of the Carnegie Corporation of New York. For example, he recommended equal financing for the education of slum children and suburban children in *Slums and Suburbs* (1961) and the creation of an Interstate Commission for Planning a Nationwide Education Policy in *Shaping Educational Policy* (1964). But at no point subsequent to 1952 did he deviate from these agenda, and at no point did he alter them significantly.[26]

Let us examine Conant's grand story, his ideas about how education works, why it goes wrong, and how it can be set right. For Conant, education clearly has social as well as intellectual goals. The mixing of youngsters from different social backgrounds with different vocational goals in comprehensive high schools is important to the continued cohesiveness and classlessness of American society, important enough to maintain in the face of the difficulty of providing a worthy education to the academically talented in the context of that mixing. Hence, the central problem for American education is how to preserve the quality of the education of the academically talented in comprehensive high schools. What goes wrong with American education is the erosion of academic standards, the slippage away from a basic curriculum of English, social studies, mathematics, and science, and the watering down of what remains of that basic curriculum. The road to making things right is the early classification of students by ability and an extensive requirement of the basics for everyone. Furthermore, making things right is a public responsibility, of public school boards and state education authorities; private schools, and particularly religious schools, in Conant's world are divisive.[27]

Within the context of the public comprehensive high school, then, and on the basis of vocational goals (and probabilities) and tests of intelligence (designed primarily to identify the 15 to 20 percent of the student body judged to be academically talented), all students should be required to take four years of English, three years of social studies (including two years of history and a senior course in American problems or American government), a year of mathematics, and a year of science. Academically talented students should be required to take, in addition to the required four years of English and three years of social studies, four years of mathematics, four years of one foreign language and ideally some additional work in another, and three years of natural science; and those students needing to develop "marketable skills" should be provided with a range of up-to-date courses and opportunities for work experience in trade, industrial, commercial, and wholesaling and retailing occupations—Conant argued that "in a heavily urbanized and industrialized free society the educational experiences of youth should fit their subsequent employment."[28]

Beyond high school, all students should have the opportunity to continue on to local junior colleges offering combinations of general and occupational education. Entry into undergraduate programs at four-year colleges and universities, however, should be restricted to the academically talented, and their curricula should be upgraded to offer more academically and professionally demanding programs. For James B. Conant popular education meant the extension of access to secondary and junior college education coupled with a narrowing and toughening of secondary school curricula, but the protection of higher education from the consequent threat of heterogeneity by contraction of enrollment and tightening of academic and professional standards. Ultimately, Conant's concern was for the training of leaders and the protection of academic traditions.

The 1960s were a time of upheaval, innovation, and radical reform at all levels of American education. I have dated the change in the climate of educational opinion from the appearance of A. S. Neill's *Summerhill* in 1960 and the rather extraordinary response it received in quarters as unlikely as the columns of *The New Yorker* and the academic communities of Cambridge and Berkeley. However that may be, the movement to "free the children," to borrow the title of Allen Graubard's thoughtful history of the free school movement, rapidly expanded to embrace the higher education sector so that by the late 1960s there were free universities as well as free schools and a plethora of alternative curricula, schools within schools, and restructured academic institutions of every sort at every level. And with the progress of the movement came changes in the grand story conveyed by the educational policy documents of the 1970s.[29]

I have alluded to the report of the Panel on Youth of the President's Science Advisory Committee (PSAC) entitled *Youth: Transition to Adulthood* as the key policy formulation of the period, though one would also have to cite two other contemporary and roughly similar formulations—namely, the report of the National Commission on the Reform of

Secondary Education (sponsored by the Charles F. Kettering Foundation) entitled *The Reform of Secondary Education*, and the report of the National Panel on High School and Adolescent Education (sponsored by the United States Office of Education) entitled *The Education of Adolescents*. All three of the committees included scholars, government officials, and practicing educators, and one, the National Commission, included a couple of high school students as well. There was virtually no overlap in the membership of the commissions: only Zahava Blum Doering, a sociologist, served with both the PSAC panel and the USOE panel. Given these facts, what was striking was the similarity in the diagnoses of the three reports and in the proposals they advanced.[30]

What were the diagnoses? In effect, they portrayed the American high school as an institution victimized by its own success: the closer it came to achieving universality, the larger, the less responsive, and the more isolated an institution it became, walling adolescents off from other segments of society, organizing them into rigidly defined age groups, and locking them into tight and inflexible academic programs. As a result, the ordinary processes by which young people became adults had become weak, confused, and disjointed—as the USOE panel phrased it, the school had decoupled the generations. Given these diagnoses, what proposals did the reports advance? In general, they urged a more flexible high school in the interest of recoupling the generations. High schools needed to be reduced in size so that students could be dealt with as individuals; curricular options needed to be broadened and diversified; arrangements needed to be made for students who wished to do so to study in other educative institutions such as libraries and museums or to gain supervised work experience in businesses or government agencies; students needed to be empowered to make more of their own decisions about their vocational and educational careers; and compulsory attendance laws and minimum-wage laws that prevented youngsters who wished to do so from getting on with their lives as adults needed to be relaxed—the National Commission advocated reducing the legal school-leaving age to fourteen so that the high schools would no longer be merely custodial institutions. Finally, in the individualistic—almost libertarian—spirit of the era, these reforms were to be undertaken by public, private, quasi-public, and combinations of private-public organizations. Given the putative inflexibility of "the system," a diversity of interests needed to be enlisted in any genuine reform.

Contemporary with the three reports on secondary education were the pronouncements of the Carnegie Commission on Higher Education established in 1967 by the Carnegie Foundation for the Advancement of Teaching. Composed primarily of businessmen and college presidents, it was led by the economist Clark Kerr, former president of the University of California. During the six years of its existence, the commission produced twenty-one separate policy documents, each more or less significant in its influence, but together constituting a formidable blueprint for the restructuring of the American higher education system. The commission announced in its very first set of recommendations released in December 1968 the theme that would sound throughout the score of reports that followed, namely, that the nation's colleges and universities needed to act energetically and even aggressively to open new channels to equality of educational opportunity and at the same time to maintain, strengthen, and protect academic quality so that America's intellectual resources would prove equal to the challenges of the modern world.[31]

How would the colleges and universities achieve these

twin goals? First, by a program of massive federal assistance to students seeking higher education and to the institutions that provided higher education. Second, by a vast expansion of local two-year community junior colleges that would reach out to high school graduates of all ages and backgrounds wishing to continue their education and offer those individuals the option of up-to-date occupational, technical, and semiprofessional courses, a wide range of general education courses to complement those vocational courses, and a variety of academic courses that would enable them to continue their education at four-year undergraduate institutions if they so desired. Third, by an equally significant expansion of so-called nontraditional education in proprietary schools, correspondence schools, work-related training programs (including those sponsored by the armed services), and various community organizations. Fourth, by a modest expansion of undergraduate programs in four-year colleges, particularly those associated with state university systems. And fifth, by carefully distinguishing between these popular commitments of higher education and what the sociologist Martin Trow called the autonomous functions of higher education—those traditional functions that the universities had historically defined for themselves, namely, the transmission of high culture, the creation of new knowledge through pure scholarship and basic scientific research, and the selection, formation, and certification of elite groups such as the learned professions and the higher civil service—and by carefully nurturing and protecting these autonomous functions from the encroachments of popular demands and sentiments.

Once again, let us examine the grand story implicit and explicit in these reports, the ideas they present about how education works, why it goes wrong, and how it can be set right. For the various commissions of the early 1970s, the popularization of education is an admirable and beneficial phenomenon, absolutely crucial to the American polity and economy. But the popularization of programs has not kept pace with the popularization of access, a problem inherent in the increasingly centralized and bureaucratized system of public education, and the result has been that the system is in a crisis—it is not working, its clients are profoundly dissatisfied and are manifesting that dissatisfaction by protest and withdrawal, and its sponsors, both public and private, are increasingly disenchanted and prone to limit their political and financial support. What needs to be done? The system needs to be reconnected with the life of society. Young people need to have a greater range of opportunities to pursue their interests and to do so in real situations in association with working adults who are not kin. More mature people need to have a greater range of opportunities to pursue their vocational and avocational interests in a variety of institutions that are accessible, welcoming, and ready to tailor education to individual needs and backgrounds. All people need to have, to paraphrase two titles of Carnegie Commission reports, a chance to learn involving more options that take less time. But there is a caveat. Certain historic functions of the universities having to do with the conduct of research, the transmission of high culture, and the creation and perpetuation of elites need to be preserved and protected from the demands of popularization, in the public interest. Popularization is all well and good, but the training of leaders who partake of high culture and occupy the key positions in the political, economic, and intellectual life of society remains all important.

The 1980s brought another shift in the climate of educational opinion, this one exemplified by the two reports that have already been alluded to, the reports of the National Commission on Excellence in Education entitled *A Nation*

at Risk, and of the Study Group on the State of Learning
in the Humanities in Higher Education entitled *To Reclaim
a Legacy.*

The National Commission had been created in 1981 by
President Reagan's first secretary of education, Terrel
Bell—the same Terrel Bell, incidentally, who in the 1970s
had introduced the report of the USOE's National Panel
on High School and Adolescent Education with a glowing
foreword referring to the report as a major contribution
to the public discussion of secondary education. The
membership of the commission included educators, scientists, businesspeople, and politicians, with David P. Gardner, president of the University of Utah, as chair (Gardner
subsequently became president of the University of California) and Yvonne W. Larsen, immediate past president
of the San Diego school board, as vice-chair. The commission held hearings, took testimony, and visited schools in
various parts of the country through much of 1982 and
then reviewed various quite different drafts of the report
during the first months of 1983. The final report—terse,
direct, and unqualified in its assertions—was largely the
work of the scientists on the panel. In effect, it put forward a severe indictment of American education and proposed a fundamental set of reforms. The report cited
rates of adult illiteracy (as many as 23 million functionally
illiterate Americans), declining scores on the Scholastic
Aptitude Test (an almost unbroken decline from 1963
to 1980), and deficiencies in knowledge on the part of
seventeen-year-olds as revealed by international tests of
achievement (American students never ranked first or second on any of nineteen academic tests). From this and
other "dimensions of the risk before us," the commission
concluded that "the educational foundations of our society are presently being eroded by a rising tide of medioc-

rity that threatens our very future as a Nation and a people."[32]

As remedies, the commission put forward five recommendations: (1) that, as a minimum, all students seeking a high school diploma be required to complete during the four years of high school the following work in the "new basics"—four years of English, three years of mathematics, three years of science, three years of social studies, and a half year of computer science; (2) that schools, colleges, and universities adopt higher expectations of their students and that four-year colleges and universities raise their requirements for admission; (3) that significantly more time be devoted to teaching and learning the new basics, and that this be achieved through more effective use of the existing school day, a lengthened school day, or a lengthened school year; (4) that the preparation of teachers be strengthened and teaching be made a more rewarding and more respected profession; and (5) that citizens throughout the nation require their elected officials to support these reforms and to provide the money necessary to achieve them. Interestingly, the report mentioned a role for the federal government in defining the national interest in education, but it assigned to state and local officials the primary responsibility for initiating and carrying out the recommendations. Beyond that, it ended with a word to parents and students, asking the parents to raise their expectations of their children, and asking students to work harder in school.[33]

During the next few years there followed in the wake of *A Nation at Risk* a score of reports on the problems of the schools, each putting forth its own particular agenda for reform. A task force organized by the Twentieth Century Fund stressed the need for English as the language of schooling, through the grades and across the country. A commission organized by the National Science Board stressed the need for all young Americans to have a firm grounding in mathematics, science, and technology. A task force organized by the Education Commission of the States stressed the relationship of more intense schooling to the maintenance of America's economic competitiveness in the world. A panel organized by the National Academy of Sciences stressed the need for academic competence in the kind of workplace that was coming into being in the United States. A task force organized by the Committee for Economic Development stressed the need for businesspeople to be interested and involved in the work of the schools. And Ernest Boyer, writing on behalf of the Carnegie Foundation for the Advancement of Teaching, stressed the need for a coherent curriculum core at the heart of any worthy secondary education. All in one way or another re-sounded the themes of *A Nation at Risk*—the need for emphasis on a new set of basics, the need for a more intensive school experience for all young people, and the need for a better trained teaching profession in the nation's schools.[34]

In addition, several major reports dealing with higher education also followed the publication of *A Nation at Risk,* notably, William J. Bennett's report on behalf of the National Endowment for the Humanities Study Group, entitled *To Reclaim a Legacy;* the report of a Select Committee of the Association of American Colleges, entitled *Integrity in the College Curriculum;* and a report of Ernest Boyer, again writing on behalf of the Carnegie Foundation for the Advancement of Teaching, entitled *College: The Undergraduate Experience in America.* All three lamented the absence of a clear vision of the educated person at the heart of undergraduate education, one that would call for all students to undertake fundamental studies in the humanities (Bennett), the natural sciences, and the social sciences (the AAC Select Committee and Boyer); all three lamented the concentration on research and the inattention to teaching in the preparation and careers of college professors; all three called for a renewed effort to develop an integrated core of required subjects that would be taught to all candidates for the bachelor's degree, whatever their majors or professional goals; and all three called for a new emphasis on imaginative and informed teaching in the nation's colleges and universities.[35]

Yet again, let us examine the grand story implicit and explicit in these reports, the ideas they present about how education works, why it goes wrong, and how it can be set right. For the various commissions of the early 1980s, the popularization of education has been an utter and complete failure, because popularization has brought with it declension and degradation. For the National Commission on Excellence in Education, the educational foundations of society are being eroded by a rising tide of mediocrity; in the National Commission's view, Paul Copperman is correct in his assertion that for the first time in the history of the United States the educational achievement of the present generation will not surpass, equal, or even approach the educational achievement of its parents. For the AAC Select Committee, a century-long decline of undergraduate education into disarray and incoherence has accompanied the rise of academic specialization associated with the research universities, and that decline has been accelerated by the upsurge of higher education enrollments since World War II. In effect, the decline and degradation have occurred because education is essentially the study of the liberal arts—what Conant called general education, what the National Commission called the new basics, what Ernest Boyer called the integrated core. The liberal arts were at the heart of education during the nineteenth and early twentieth centuries, and popularization has brought a vitiation of their formative power in favor of narrow specialization and crass vocationalism. How can education be set right? By requiring study of the liberal arts of all students, and by popularizing education without permitting it to be vulgarized, that is, by universalizing precisely the education that was formerly preserved for the few and making it mandatory for all. The popularization of education involves an increase in the size of the clientele, not a transformation in the nature of the curriculum.

Nowhere was the grand story of the early 1980s more dramatically presented than in Allan Bloom's *The Closing of the American Mind.* The educational and political crisis of twentieth-century America is essentially an intellectual crisis, Bloom asserted. It derives, he continued, from the university's lack of central purpose, from the students' lack of fundamental learning, from the displacement of the traditional classical humanistic works that long dominated the curriculum—the works of Plato and Aristotle and Augustine and Shakespeare and Spinoza and Rousseau—by specialized electives and courses in the creative arts, and from the triumph of relativism over perennial humanistic values. How can the crisis be resolved? Clearly, by a restoration of true learning in the schools and colleges through the traditional disciplines and the works of the Western canon. Could that restoration be compatible with further popularization of higher education? Almost certainly not!

V

My friend Richard Heffner once asked me on his television program, *The Open Mind,* whether the ideal of popular education was not an impossible ideal, whether it not only was not working but in the end could not work. I maintained that no ideal is ever completely achievable; if it is, it is not an ideal. What an ideal does hold out is a goal, which people can then approach more or less successfully. And I argued that the ideal of popular education, at least as it had developed in the United States, was one of the most radical ideals in the Western world, that we had made great progress in moving toward the ideal, but that the attainment had been wanting in many domains, and that the institutions we had established to further that attainment had been flawed in many respects. We had, to be blunt, a long way to go, but it was worth trying to get there.

After we were off the air, I asked Heffner if he was not really asking whether the phrase popular education is an oxymoron, a contradiction, in its very nature flawed and unachievable. He protested not. But I think many people believe that the contradiction is there, that education in its true meaning is an elite phenomenon, just as such people would argue that culture in its true meaning is an elite phenomenon, and that as soon as education begins to be transformed by popularization—by popular interest, popular demand, popular understanding, and popular acceptance—it is inevitably vulgarized. In essence, these people would argue that there is no more possibility of a popular education than there is of a popular culture. What results when education is popularized is an educational version of what the critic Dwight Macdonald once labeled "masscult" or "midcult." I believe this is the explicit message of Allan Bloom's book. And I would trace the most fundamental and abiding discontent with popular education in the United States to the sense that it is not only an impossible ideal but in the end a hopeless contradiction.[36]

To argue in favor of popular education is not to deny the tremendous difficulties inevitably involved in achieving it. On the one side, there are the inescapable political problems of determining the nature, content, and values of popular education. Legislators want the schools to teach the advantages of patriotism and the dangers of substance abuse; parents want the schools to teach character and discipline; employers want the schools to teach diligence and the basic skills; arts advocates want the schools to teach painting, drama, music, and dance; academics want the schools to teach more of what they know—historians want more history, mathematicians more mathematics, and economists more economics; students want the schools to equip them to go on to college if they wish, to prepare them to obtain and hold a job with a future, and to offer them opportunities to enjoy sports, hobbies, and a decent social life; and a host of organized citizens' groups want the schools to attend to their special concerns, which range from civil liberties to fire prevention. Out of a process that involves all three branches of government at the state and federal levels as well as thousands of local school boards, a plethora of private interests ranging from publishers to accrediting agencies, and the variety of professionals who actually operate the schools emerges what we call the curriculum, with its requirements, its electives, its informal activities, and its unacknowledged routines. It is that curriculum, in various versions, that is supposed to be offered to all the children of all the people. On the other side, there are the demands of the children, with their almost infinite variety of needs, wants, and values, deriving from extraordinary differences in their family backgrounds, their rates and patterns of development, their learning styles, and their social, intellectual, and vocational aspirations.

The resulting dilemmas are as difficult philosophically as they are insistent politically. Will the increased stringency of academic requirements stimulated by the report of the National Commission on Excellence in Education create a rise in the dropout rate at the same time that it encourages more capable students to higher levels of academic performance? The dropout rate has indeed gone up, but we do not know whether that testifies to the inability (or unwillingness) of students to master the newly required material or the difficulties teachers face in teaching the newly required material with sufficient versatility, or both. However that may be, the loss to the American polity, economy, and society, and to the individual youngsters who drop out, is prodigious. Meanwhile, the Japanese, though admittedly a less heterogeneous people than the Americans, are mandating even more difficult material for their high school students, with a lower dropout rate. Will the effort to advance racial integration by insisting upon comprehensive high schools cause white flight that in the end leads to increased segregation and lower academic performance? There are those who say that it will, and there are communities where the effort to maintain comprehensive high schools has been correlated with white flight, increased segregation, and lower academic performance. Meanwhile, the Swedes seem to be managing to maintain comprehensive high schools in an increasingly heterogeneous society without lowering academic performance. Do the traditions of competitive individualism lead American parents, teachers, and students to assume that some young people must inevitably fail? The data from John Goodlad's study of schooling provide evidence that such assumptions are rampant. Yet there have long been experimental schools in the United States and abroad in which the school class as a whole has been made responsible for the performance of individual members, with the result that students end up helping one another to succeed. In sum, does the success of popular education ultimately depend upon the values of the society it is meant to nurture and sustain, which in the

American case involves a penchant for utility, an ambivalence toward book learning, and a preoccupation with individual success? Do such values by their very nature compromise the success of popular education?[37]

Furthermore, there are the patent flaws in the system of institutions Americans have created to realize the ideal of popular education. One might note in the first place the undetermined number of children in the United States who are simply not in school at any given time for one reason or another and who are not even known to be not in school. When the Children's Defense Fund did its pioneering study of *Children Out of School in America* during the early 1970s, it found, quite beyond the United States census statistic of nearly two million children between the ages of seven and seventeen out of school, thousands of children who had been expelled or suspended for disciplinary reasons, countless truants who had managed to elude census enumerators and attendance officers, and undetermined numbers of children who had fallen through the cracks of the system for reasons of pregnancy, poverty, mental retardation, or emotional disability. In addition, it found even greater numbers of children who were technically in school but who might just as well have been counted as out of school—youngsters of recent immigrant families sitting uncomprehendingly in classrooms conducted in English, youngsters misdiagnosed as retarded who were really deaf, youngsters so alienated by real or perceived indifference, condescension, or prejudice that they had long since stopped profiting from anything the schools had to offer.[38]

One might go on to note the flaws in individual institutions—elementary schools where children do not learn to read because they are not taught; high schools where young men and women from working-class backgrounds are denied access to the studies of languages and mathematics

that would make it possible for them to become engineers
or scientists; junior colleges where recent immigrants with
aspirations to undergraduate degrees cannot find the guid-
ance they require to choose the proper academic courses
and hence end up locked into narrow occupational programs; and four-year colleges where students graduating
with a mélange of "gut" courses find themselves with a
worthless credential and few prospects of decent employment. One might note, too, the flaws in whole systems of
schooling, especially the overbureaucratized and under-
financed systems of many of our central cities, heavily
populated by the poor, the nonwhite, and the recently arrived, those most in need of carefully and expertly delivered educational services and least likely to receive them.

Popular education, then, is as radical an ideal as Americans have embraced. It is by its very nature fraught with
difficulty, and the institutions we have established to
achieve it are undeniably flawed. Yet it is important to be
aware of what has been accomplished in the movement
toward popular education and of the possibilities for the
future. I believe the predicament of American schooling
during the early 1980s was not nearly so dire as the report
of the National Commission suggested. As Lawrence Stedman and Marshall Smith pointed out in a detailed examina-
tion of the evidence cited in the report, the academic
achievement of young Americans in the early 1980s was far
more mixed than the commission alleged. There were
definite improvements in the performance of younger children, reflecting, I believe, the additional educational services made available by Title I/Chapter I federal funds.
These were coupled with a patently uneven performance
on the part of adolescents, a performance marked by relatively good showings in literature and the social studies and
rather poor showings in foreign languages, mathematics,

and the natural sciences as well as in the development of the higher order skills associated with critical thinking. Everyone agreed that the results should have been better—in fact, there were data in John Goodlad's study of schooling suggesting that significant numbers of the students themselves believed they might have been working harder and more effectively. Moreover, given the extraordinary percentage of young Americans who were continuing on to postsecondary education, the results would likely have been better in comparison with other countries had the tests been administered at age nineteen or twenty instead of seventeen or eighteen. However that may be, there was surely no evidence to support the commission's affirmation of Paul Copperman's claim that the present generation would be the first in American history whose educational skills would not equal or even approach those of its parents.[39]

Furthermore, we know that standardized tests measure at best only a fraction of what young people have learned in school, and they measure that imperfectly, so that if one were to venture past the test scores to examine what was actually happening in the schools of the early 1980s, a cluster of studies by scholars like John Goodlad, Philip Jackson, Sara Lawrence Lightfoot, Mary Haywood Metz, Vito Perrone, Arthur Powell, and others revealed a far more complex picture of what was going on. They indicated that, overall, there was strong emphasis in school curricula on the English language and literature; that considerable importance was being placed on social studies, mathematics, the natural sciences, the arts, physical education, and, in the upper grades, so-called career education but that foreign languages were receiving limited attention at best; that teachers were mindful of their responsibility to inculcate discipline and nurture civic and social skills; that most

schools were orderly places where teachers and students
went about the diurnal business of education in a systematic
and mutually respectful fashion; that many schools were
contending thoughtfully and effectively with the prodigious
problems of integrating vastly diverse clienteles into the
American polity and economy; that students in general
were learning what their parents and teachers thought it
was important for them to learn; and that there were significant numbers of students who excelled, by any reasonable
standard, in literature, the sciences, the fine and perform-
ing arts, and athletics. But they also indicated that students
spent less time in school each year and less time at home
doing schoolwork than their counterparts in a number of
other countries; that teachers, particularly at the elementary level, were poorly trained in mathematics and the natural sciences and that their poor training was a key factor in
the relatively low achievement of students in those subjects;
that far too much teaching was uninspired and unimaginative, with consistent overreliance on lectures, drills, and
workbooks and underreliance on a wide range of alternative pedagogies and technologies; that teachers felt
severely constrained in their daily work by bureaucratic
rules and procedures; and, most important, that the greatest failures and most serious unsolved problems of the system were those relating to the education of poor children
from minority populations in the schools of the central
cities.[40]

The reports on higher education during the 1980s, with
their emphasis on the loss of an integrated core in undergraduate education and the deleterious effects of that loss,
were also at best distorted in their diagnosis of the current
situation. Whatever core there might have been in the liberal arts institutions of the seventeenth and eighteenth centuries had already begun to disintegrate in the nineteenth

century in the face of rising enrollments and expanding commitments, and with the exception of its presence in a few elite colleges and universities, that core as traditionally defined has not been much seen in the twentieth century. The explosion of knowledge that marked the rise of the research university necessitated not only the extensive choice embodied in the elective system but also the kind of continuing redefinition of any integrated core by college and university faculties that would inevitably lead to various versions of general and liberal education. Allan Bloom's Western canon is one of those versions, but only one. There are other versions that derive from different definitions of the educated person.

That variety of definitions holds the key, it seems to me, to the current situation in American education. Americans have traditionally assigned a wide range of responsibilities to their schools and colleges. They want the schools and colleges to teach the fundamental skills of reading, writing, and arithmetic; to nurture critical thinking; to convey a general fund of knowledge; to develop creativity and aesthetic perception; to assist students in choosing and preparing for vocations in a highly complex economy; to inculcate ethical character and good citizenship; to develop physical and emotional well-being; and to nurture the ability, the intelligence, and the will to continue on with education as far as any particular individual wants to go. And this catalogue does not even mention such herculean social tasks as taking the initiative in racial desegregation and informing the population about the dangers of drug abuse and AIDS. Americans have also maintained broad notions of the active intellect and informed intelligence required to participate responsibly in the affairs of American life. One associates these notions with the inclusive definitions of literacy that make the role of literacy in everyday life central and with the plural definitions of intelligence that embrace musical and kinesthetic intelligence as well as logical, linguistic, and mathematical intelligence—the sorts of definitions that Howard Gardner has advanced in *Frames of Mind* (1983). And they have not only countenanced but urged a wide-ranging curriculum that goes far beyond the "new basics" or the "integrated core" or the "Western canon" of the recent policy reports—those are at best somewhat narrow, academicist versions of American education. As with all latitudinarianism, such definitions can permit triviality to enter the curriculum, and triviality is not difficult to find in American schools and colleges. But on balance I believe such broad definitions have served the American people well.[41]

If there is a crisis in American schooling, it is not the crisis of putative mediocrity and decline charged by the recent reports but rather the crisis inherent in balancing this tremendous variety of demands Americans have made on their schools and colleges—of crafting curricula that take account of the needs of a modern society at the same time that they make provision for the extraordinary diversity of America's young people; of designing institutions where well-prepared teachers can teach under supportive conditions, and where *all* students can be motivated and assisted to develop their talents to the fullest; and of providing the necessary resources for creating and sustaining such institutions. These tough problems may not make it into the headlines or onto television, and there is no quick fix that will solve them; but in the end they constitute the real and abiding crisis of popular schooling in the United States.

In thinking about the search for solutions, it is well to bear in mind that there remain some 15,000 school districts in the United States that sponsor about 59,000 elementary schools and 24,000 secondary schools, and that there are also almost 21,000 private elementary schools and 8,000 private secondary schools. In addition, there are around 3,000 institutions of higher education, of which fully a third are two-year community colleges. Given this multitude of institutions organized into fifty state systems—some highly centralized, some loosely decentralized—programs of education will differ, and local as well as cosmopolitan influences will prevail. For all the centralizing tendencies in American schooling—from federal mandates to regional accrediting association guidelines to standardized tests and textbooks—the experience students have in one school will differ from the experience they have in another, whatever the formal curriculum indicates might be going on; and the standards by which we judge those experiences will derive from local realities, clienteles, faculties, and aspirations as well as from cosmopolitan knowledge, norms, and expectations. The good school, as Sara Lightfoot has argued, is good in its context.[42]

It is that point, I believe, that the high school reports of the 1970s were trying to make, when they recommended the further differentiation of curricula and the brokering by the schools of educational opportunities for youngsters in libraries, museums, workplaces, government agencies, and community organizations. It is that point, too, that the Carnegie Commission was trying to make when it recommended a vast expansion of enrollments and a further diversification of curricula in the first two years of post-secondary education. Where I would quarrel with the Carnegie Commission (and later the Carnegie Council on Policy Studies in Higher Education) would be in its insistence on confining the expansion and diversification to the junior college and on protecting the four-year colleges from the demands and effects of popularization. In my own view, the commission drew far too great a distinction between the programs of two-year and four-year colleges and invested far too much energy in trying to preserve the imagined distinctions. For one thing, there is tremendous overlap in the character of the two kinds of institutions. For another, both need adjustment to facilitate the easy transfer of students from the former to the latter, which was envisioned by President Truman's Commission on Higher Education, but which has not come to pass.

More important, however, I believe there is need for a far greater sense of unity in the American school system, one that envisions the system whole, extending from nursery schools through the so-called doctorate-granting institutions, with individuals making their way through the system according to their own lights and aspirations and institutions creating their clienteles competitively, much as they do today. I would abandon the constraint the Carnegie Commission preached when it expressed the hope that the two-year colleges would be discouraged from trying to become four-year undergraduate institutions. Sir Eric Ashby, who prepared the immensely incisive monograph *Any Person, Any Study* for the Carnegie Commission—the title bespoke Sir Eric's sense of the openness of American higher education—observed that while the Soviet Union maintained a diversity of higher education institutions stratified according to subjects the United States maintained a diversity of higher education institutions stratified according to quality. He defined quality, of course, in terms of what Martin Trow had called the "autonomous" functions of higher education—with the elite universities devoted primarily to research at the top, with the comprehensive universities dividing their efforts between research and teaching at a somewhat lower status, and with the colleges and universities devoting their efforts primarily to teaching occupying an even lower status. I would alter Ashby's aphorism to argue that while the Soviet Union maintains a diversity of higher education institutions stratified according to subjects the United States maintains a diversity of higher education institutions organized according to missions, missions that vary considerably. And I think that kind of organization is part of the genius of American education—it provides a place for everybody who wishes one, and in the end yields one of the most educated populations in the world.[43]

NOTES

1. Thomas D. Snyder, *Digest of Education Statistics, 1987* (Washington, D.C.: Government Printing Office, 1987), 13.

2. National Commission on Excellence in Education, *A Nation at Risk: The Imperative for Educational Reform* (Washington, D.C.: GPO, 1983), 5.

3. Philadelphia *National Gazette*, July 10, 1830, 2; [Frederick Adolphus Packard], *The Daily Public School in the United States* (Philadelphia: Lippincott, 1866), 10–11; J. F. Cooper, *Notions of the Americans* (2 vols.; London: Henry Colburn, 1828), 2:122, 127; and Alexis de Tocqueville, *Democracy in America*, edited by Phillips Bradley (2 vols.; New York: Knopf, 1945), 1:315.

4. Lys d'Aimée, "The Menace of Present Educational Methods," *Gunton's Magazine*, 19 (September 1900):263; and Lawrence A. Cremin and Robert M. Weiss, "Yesterday's School Critic," *Teachers College Record*, 54 (November 1952):77–82.

5. Irving Babbitt, *Literature and the American College: Essays in Defense of the Humanities* (Boston: Houghton Mifflin, 1908), chap. 3; Abraham Flexner, *A Modern College and a Modern School* (Garden City, N. Y.: Doubleday, Page, 1923), *Do Americans Really Value Education?* (Cambridge, Mass.: Harvard University Press, 1927), and *Universities: American, English, German* (New York: Oxford University Press, 1930); and Robert Maynard Hutchins, *The Higher Learning in America* (New Haven: Yale University Press, 1936).

6. Michael E. Sadler, "Impressions of American Education," *Educational Review*, 25 (March 1903):228; and Erich Hylla, *Die Schule der Demokratie: Ein Aufriss des Bildungswesens der Vereinigten Staaten* (Langensalza: Verlag von Julius Beltz, 1928), chap. 3.

7. Arthur Bestor, *The Restoration of Learning: A Program for Redeeming the Unfulfilled Promise of American Education* (New York: Knopf, 1955); H. G. Rickover, *Education and Freedom* (New York: Dutton, 1959); Hutchins, *Higher Learning in America;* Harold J. Laski, *The American Democracy: A Commentary and an Interpretation* (New York: Viking, 1948), chap. 8; and D. W. Brogan, *The American Character* (New York: Knopf, 1944), 137.

8. Paul Copperman, *The Literacy Hoax: The Decline of Reading, Writing, and Learning in the Public Schools and What We Can Do About It* (New York: Morrow, 1978), and "The Achievement Decline of the 1970's," *Phi Delta Kappan,* 60 (June 1979):736–739; National Commission on Excellence in Education, *A Nation at Risk,* 11; and Allan Bloom, *The Closing of the American Mind* (New York: Simon and Schuster, 1987).

9. Hutchins, *Higher Learning in America,* 70, 85, and *passim;* and John Dewey, *The Way Out of Educational Confusion* (Cambridge, Mass.: Harvard University Press, 1931).

10. James S. Coleman and Thomas Hoffer, *Public and Private Schools: The Impact of Communities* (New York: Basic Books, 1987), chap. 8.

11. John U. Ogbu, *Minority Education and Caste: The American System in Cross-Cultural Perspective* (New York: Academic Press, 1978), and "Cultural Discontinuities and Schooling," *Anthropology and Education Quarterly,* 13 (Winter 1982):290–307.

12. Alvin Toffler, *The Culture Consumers: A Study of Art and Affluence in America* (New York: St. Martin's Press, 1964). A kindred argument is advanced by David K. Cohen and Barbara Neufeld in "The Failure of High Schools and the Progress of Education," *Daedalus,* 110 (Summer 1981):69–89.

13. The report of the National Geographic Society's press conference is carried in the *New York Times,* July 28, 1988, A16.

14. Snyder, *Digest of Education Statistics, 1987,* 13; and U. S., Office of Education, Division of Educational Statistics, *Digest of Educational Statistics,* 1962, (Washington, D. C.: GPO, 1962), 12.

15. Leonard P. Ayres, *Laggards in Our Schools: A Study of Retardation and Elimination in City School Systems* (New York: Russell Sage Foundation, 1909), chap. 9.

16. George S. Counts, *The Selective Character of American Secondary Education* (Chicago: University of Chicago Press, 1922); and M. S. Katz, *A History of Compulsory Education Laws* (Bloomington: The Phi Delta Kappa Educational Foundation, 1976), 22.

17. Educational Policies Commission, *Education for ALL American Youth* (Washington, D.C.: National Education Association, 1944).

18. *Higher Education for American Democracy: A Report of the President's Commission on Higher Education* (5 vols.; New York: Harper & Brothers, 1948), 1:101, 69.

19. Snyder, *Digest of Education Statistics, 1987,* 50, 83, 12, 13; and Garland G. Parker, *The Enrollment Explosion: A Half-Century of Attendance in U.S. Colleges and Universities* (New York: School & Society Books, 1971), chaps. 3–5.

20. Vincent Tinto, *Leaving College: Rethinking the Causes and Cures of Student Attrition* (Chicago: University of Chicago Press, 1987), 18–19; and Kevin Dougherty, "The Effects of Community Colleges: Aid or Hindrance to Socio-

economic Attainment?" *Sociology of Education,* 60 (April 1987):86–103. See also Karl L. Alexander, Scott Holupka, and Aaron M. Pallas, "Social Background and Academic Determinants of Two-Year Versus Four-Year College Attendance: Evidence from Two Cohorts a Decade Apart," *American Journal of Education,* 96 (November 1987):56–80; and William Velez and Rajshekhar G. Javelgi, "Two-Year College to Four-Year College: The Likelihood of Transfer," ibid., 81–94.

21. JB Lon Hefferlin, *Dynamics of Academic Reform* (San Francisco: Jossey-Bass, 1969), chap. 3.

22. Ruth B. Ekstrom, Margaret E. Goertz, Judith M. Pollack, and Donald A. Rock, "Who Drops Out of High School and Why? Findings From a National Study," *Teachers College Record,* 87 (Spring 1987):363–364; and Michelle Fine, "Why Urban Adolescents Drop into and out of Public High School," ibid., 394–409.

23. Arthur W. Chickering and William Hannah, "The Process of Withdrawal," *Liberal Education,* 55 (December 1969):551–558; Robert J. Panos and Alexander W. Astin, "Attrition Among College Students," *American Educational Research Journal,* 5 (January 1968):57–72; Carnegie Foundation for the Advancement of Teaching, *Missions of the College Curriculum: A Contemporary Review with Suggestions* (San Francisco: Jossey-Bass, 1977), 91–92; and Tinto, *Leaving College.* See also Robert Cope and William Hannah, *Revolving College Doors: The Causes and Consequences of Dropping Out, Stopping Out, and Transferring* (New York: Wiley, 1975).

24. David K. Cohen and Michael S. Garet, "Reforming Educational Policy with Applied Social Research," *Harvard Educational Review,* 45 (February 1975):21.

25. James Bryant Conant and Francis Spaulding, *Education for a Classless Society* (Cambridge, Mass.: Harvard University Press, 1940).

26. James Bryant Conant, *Education and Liberty: The Role of Schools in a Modern Democracy* (Cambridge, Mass.: Harvard University Press, 1953), 57–58, *Slums and Suburbs: A Commentary on Schools in Metropolitan Areas* (New York: McGraw-Hill, 1961), and *Shaping Educational Policy* (New York: McGraw-Hill, 1964). For the context of Conant's writings on educational policy, see Ellen Condliffe Lagemann, *The Politics of Knowledge: The Carnegie Corporation, Philanthropy, and Public Policy* (Middletown: Wesleyan University Press, 1989), chap. 8.

27. Conant, *Education and Liberty,* 81.

28. James Bryant Conant, *The American High School Today: A First Report to Interested Citizens* (New York: McGraw-Hill, 1959), section 3, and *Slums and Suburbs,* 40.

29. Allen Graubard, *Free the Children: Radical Reform and the Free School Movement* (New York: Pantheon Books, 1972).

30. Panel on Youth of the President's Science Advisory Committee, *Youth: Transition to Adulthood* (Washington, D.C.: GPO, 1973); National Commission on the Reform of Secondary Education, *The Reform of Secondary Education: A Report to the Public and the Profession* (New York: McGraw-Hill, 1973); and National Panel on High School and Adolescent Education, *The Education of Adolescents* (Washington, D.C.: U. S. Office of Education, 1974).

31. Carnegie Commission on Higher Education, *Quality and Equality: New Levels of Federal Responsibility for Higher Education* (New York: McGraw-Hill,

1968), and *A Digest of Reports of the Carnegie Commission on Higher Education* (New York: McGraw-Hill, 1974). For the context of the work of the commission, see Ellen Condliffe Lagemann, *Private Power for the Public Good: A History of the Carnegie Foundation for the Advancement of Teaching* (Middletown: Wesleyan University Press, 1983), chap. 6.

32. National Commission on Excellence in Education, *A Nation at Risk,* 8–11, 5.

33. *Ibid.,* 24–33.

34. Twentieth Century Fund Task Force on Federal Elementary and Secondary Education Policy, *Making the Grade* (New York: The Twentieth Century Fund, 1983); National Science Board Commission on Precollegiate Education in Mathematics, Science, and Technology, *Educating Americans for the 21st Century: A Plan of Action for Improving Mathematics, Science, and Technology Education for All American Elementary and Secondary Students So That Their Achievement Is the Best in the World by 1995* (Washington, D.C.: National Science Foundation, 1983); Education Commission of the States, Task Force on Education for Economic Growth, *Action for Excellence: A Comprehensive Plan to Improve Our Nation's Schools* (Washington, D.C.: Education Commission of the States, 1983); National Academy of Sciences, Committee on Science, Engineering, and Public Policy, Panel on Secondary School Education for the Changing Workplace, *High Schools and the Changing Workplace: The Employers' View* (Washington, D.C.: National Academy Press, 1984); Committee for Economic Development, Research and Policy Committee, *Investing in Our Children: Business and the Public Schools* (New York: Committee for Economic Development, 1985); and Ernest L. Boyer, *High School: A Report on Secondary Education in America* (New York: Harper & Row, 1983).

35. William J. Bennett, *To Reclaim a Legacy: A Report on the Humanities in Higher Education* (Washington, D.C.: National Endowment for the Humanities, 1984); Association of American Colleges, Project on Defining the Meaning and Purpose of Baccalaureate Degrees, *Integrity in the College Curriculum: A Report to the Academic Community* (Washington, D.C.: Association of American Colleges, 1985); and Ernest L. Boyer, *College: The Undergraduate Experience in America* (New York: Harper & Row, 1987).

36. Dwight Macdonald, *Against the American Grain* (New York: Random House, 1962), part 1.

37. With respect to the prodigious costs of continuing high dropout rates, one might note the argument of Margaret D. LeCompte and Anthony Gary Dworkin: "Given the indirect link between education and poverty, we believe that a significant measure of the success of an educational innovation, whether enriching or compensatory, is not whether the student test scores rise, but whether it improves the retention of an entire cohort of students and faculty," in "Educational Programs: Indirect Linkages and Unfulfilled Expectations," in Harrell R. Rodgers, Jr., ed., *Beyond Welfare: New Approaches to the Problem of Poverty in America* (Armonk, N. Y.: Sharpe, 1988), 136. For some of the Goodlad evidence, see Kenneth A. Tye, *The Junior High: School in Search of a Mission* (Lankam, Md.: University Press of America, 1985), 1–2.

38. Children's Defense Fund, *Children out of School in America* (Washington, D. C.: Children's Defense Fund, 1974).

39. Lawrence C. Stedman and Marshall S. Smith, "Recent Reform Proposals for American Education," *Contemporary Education Review,* 2 (Fall 1983):85–

104. See also Ralph W. Tyler, "The U.S. vs. the World: A Comparison of Educational Performance," *Phi Delta Kappan*, 62 (January 1981): 307–310, Gilbert R. Austin and Herbert Garber, eds., *The Rise and Fall of National Test Scores* (New York: Academic Press, 1982), and, for a later summary of the test data, U. S. Congress, Congressional Budget Office, *Trends in Educational Achievement* (April 1986) and *Educational Achievement: Explanations and Implications of Recent Trends* (August 1987). John I. Goodlad, *A Place Called School: Prospects for the Future* (New York: McGraw-Hill, 1984), chap. 3 and *passim*, and Barbara Benham Tye, *Multiple Realities: A Study of 13 American High Schools* (Lanham, N.Y.: University Press of America, 1985), chap. 4 and *passim*.

40. Goodlad, *A Place Called School;* Stephen R. Graubard, ed., "America's Schools: Portraits and Perspectives," *Daedalus*, 110 (Fall 1981); Sara Lawrence Lightfoot, *The Good High School: Portraits of Character and Culture* (New York: Basic Books, 1983); Mary Haywood Metz, *Different by Design: The Context and Character of Three Magnet Schools* (New York: Routledge & Kegan Paul, 1986); Jeannie Oakes, *Keeping Track: How Schools Structure Inequality* (New Haven: Yale University Press, 1985); Vito Perrone et al., *Portraits of High Schools* (Princeton, N. J.: The Carnegie Foundation for the Advancement of Teaching, 1985); Barbara Benham Tye, *Multiple Realities;* Kenneth A. Tye, *The Junior High*, and Arthur G. Powell, Eleanor Farrar, and David K. Cohen, *The Shopping Mall High School: Winners and Losers in the Educational Marketplace* (Boston: Houghton Mifflin, 1985).

For an early warning against using the international studies of educational achievement as some kind of "international contest," see Torsten Husén, ed., *International Study of Achievement in Mathematics: A Comparison of Twelve Countries* (2 vols.; New York: Wiley, 1967), 2:288, and *passim*. For a review of the uses and limitations of standardized paper-and-pencil tests as instruments for assessing what is learned in school, see Bernard R. Gifford, ed., *Test Policy and Test Performance: Education, Language, and Culture* (Boston: Kluwer, 1989), Bernard R. Gifford and M. Catherine O'Connor, eds., *New Approaches to Testing: Rethinking Aptitude, Achievement, and Assessment* (Boston: Kluwer, 1990), and other publications reporting the work of the National Commission on Testing and Public Policy.

41. The list of responsibilities assigned to the schools and colleges is based on John I. Goodlad's study of schooling, as reported in *What Schools Are For* (Bloomington, Ind.: Phi Delta Kappa Educational Foundation, 1979) and *A Place Called School*, and Ernest L. Boyer's study of the undergraduate experience, as reported in *College*.

42. Lightfoot, *The Good High School*.

43. Eric Ashby, *Any Person, Any Study: An Essay on Higher Education in the United States* (New York: McGraw-Hill, 1971); and Martin Trow, "Reflections on the Transition from Mass to Universal Higher Education," *Daedalus*, 99 (Winter 1970):1–7.

THE CACOPHONY
OF TEACHING

The electronic environment makes an information level outside the schoolroom that is far higher than the information
level inside the schoolroom. In the nineteenth century the
knowledge inside the schoolroom was higher than knowledge outside the schoolroom. Today it is reversed. The
child knows that in going to school he is in a sense interrupt-
ing his education.   —H. MARSHALL MCLUHAN,
                                      "NBC Experiment in Television,"
                                              March 19, 1967

I

The popularization of schooling following World War II
went forward in a context of rapid social change that radically transformed the ecology of education in the United
States and fundamentally altered the circumstances within
which schools and colleges carried on their work. That
change was compounded of many elements—the successive
waves of immigration from Central and South America,
from Africa and the Middle East, and from South and
Southeast Asia; the great internal migrations from country
to city, from city to suburb, from the Midwest to the two
coasts, and from the rust belt to the sun belt; unceasing
technological development in every phase of American life,
from industrial production to political bureaucracy; the
powerful civil rights movements of the 1960s and the grow-

ing general demand for equity throughout the society; and the emergence of a global economy and the exploration of outer space. But I should like to focus on two elements that I believe were directly transformative of education in its own right and that quite literally shook schooling to its very foundations: I refer, first, to the profound changes in the rearing of children and, second, to the sweeping changes in the nature, uses, and delivery of information throughout the society.

The changes in the rearing of children flowed, of course, from changes in the structure, composition, and character of American families. American families expanded for a time after 1945 but then began a steady decline in size during the 1960s, reflecting smaller numbers of adults and children in the average household. Of family households enumerated in the 1980 census, 82 percent comprised four or fewer members. American families also became less and less stable after 1965 as rates of divorce rose rapidly to a point where in 1979 there were twenty-three divorces for every thousand existing marriages. One result was that by the early 1980s one out of four parents under the age of 25 listed as head of a household was living without a spouse, and one out of five children under the age of eighteen was living in a single-parent household. American families were also more variegated, as some five to seven million people came to the United States during the 1970s, mostly from the Caribbean, Latin America, and South and Southeast Asia. And American families were increasingly dual-career families, as the percentage of women in the labor force rose from 33.9 in 1940 to 51.9 in 1980 and as the percentage of married women in the labor force whose youngest child was under the age of six rose from 12 in 1950 to almost 50 in 1980 (looked at from the perspective of the children, 54 percent of all children under the age of eighteen in 1981 had mothers in the labor force, as did 45 percent of all preschoolers).[1]

Now, there are several points to be made here about education. For one thing, the family is the institution in which children have their earliest education, their earliest experiences in the learning of languages, the nurturance of cognitive, emotional, and motor competences, the maintenance of interpersonal relationships, the internalization of values, and the assignment of meaning to the world. Furthermore, the family is the institution within which children first develop what my colleague Hope Jensen Leichter has called their educative styles—their characteristic ways of engaging in, moving through, and combining educative experiences over the lifespan. Given the changes in the structure, composition, and character of American families since World War II, and particularly during the past two decades, one would have reason to expect a far greater range and diversity of early education—to wit, a far greater range and diversity of languages, competences, values, personalities, and approaches to the world and to its educational opportunities.[2]

Differences such as these have been compounded by at least three additional developments, namely, the entry of television broadcasting into the nation's households, the direct address of much of that broadcasting to adolescent audiences, and the expansion of home and institutional day care as responses to the increasing number of dual-career families. I shall comment on television broadcasting at greater length later, but it is important for an understanding of familial education to note that television is watched primarily in the home in the United States and that, insofar as television educates, its influence is exerted in the context of familial education. As for the direct address of television broadcasting to adolescent audiences, often referred to as markets, it has in many ways strengthened the bonds of the adolescent peer group, which has exercised an increasingly powerful educative influence during the past half century. The Lynds in their classic Middletown studies took note as early as the 1920s of the rise of the adolescent peer group as a significant educative influence; and Theodore Caplow and his associates in the more recent replication of the Middletown studies noted the increasing amounts of time allocated to television viewing. When adolescents are seen as a special market—particularly for distinctive music, foods, clothing, and cosmetics—factors making for a separate adolescent society, already somewhat discrete from adult society, are strengthened, and the potential for conflict between the values and attitudes of that society and parental values and attitudes is heightened. What I have good-humoredly referred to over the years as the "Pinocchio Effect"—the effect of companions seen by parents as "bad company"—is thereby strengthened.[3]

As for day care, the trends have been clear and unmistakable. In 1958 slightly over half of all mothers in the labor force relied on day care in the home; by 1982 that proportion had dropped to about a quarter. Use of day care in another home rose from 27 to 44 percent, while use of day care centers outside the home rose from 4 to 19 percent among mothers employed full time. We know too little about the character and effects of home and institutional day care. A good deal of institutional day care is provided by the churches and synagogues, some by commercial enterprises, and a little by employers, though, faced with increasing competition for capable workers, employers are gradually creating or expanding day care facilities as an enhancement to their employee benefits packages. We also know that day care centers can be conducted with very different ends in mind, from custody to recreation to social and educational development. We know even less about the interaction of particular kinds of day care with particular kinds of familial education, though one would expect the permutations and combinations to lead to further diversity rather than further standardization.[4]

Mention of the churches and synagogues calls to mind one additional point that is crucial to understand with reference to the ecology of education, namely, that church and synagogue congregations are essentially gatherings of families and that churches and synagogues exercise much of their educative influence through families and in concert with families. The Congress of National Black Churches built its Project SPIRIT on this insight, with excellent results. The teachers and administrators of predominantly black schools in cities as different as Oakland, Indianapolis, and Atlanta have worked closely with the congregations and ministers of the black churches in those cities in an effort to instill in children the qualities of strength, perseverance, imagination, responsibility, integrity, and talent (hence, the acronym SPIRIT) that will assist them in their quest for education and for satisfying lives. The insight, of course, is scarcely limited to black churches and congregations; one sees it at work in a host of arrangements worked out by religious groups as different as fundamentalist Christians, conservative Jews, and recently arrived Vietnamese Buddhists.[5]

With respect to the sweeping changes in the nature, uses, and delivery of information in the United States, there are two points I should like to emphasize, among many that might be made. The first concerns the rise of popular television broadcasting since World War II; the second concerns the nature of work in the emerging American economy and the locus of education for work. Television viewing became virtually ubiquitous in the United States in the years following World War II. In 1950 television was in roughly 10 percent of American homes; by the early 1980s it was in 97 to 98 percent of American homes, frequently conveyed on two, three, or four sets, and watched on the average of seven hours a day, mostly by the very young, the very old, and the very poor. Television entertains, it diverts, it engages, it fills time, and it provides background for countless household activities. Whatever else it does, however, it educates and miseducates relentlessly. It conveys information and knowledge through news programs and documentaries; it creates wants through commercials; and it offers models of behavior through soap operas and sitcoms.

Television has also demonstrated an impressive ability to carry out formal teaching. If we take the work of the Children's Television Workshop as an example, the ability of television programming to teach the alphabet, numbers, and certain well-accepted values to preschoolers has been decisively demonstrated by *Sesame Street;* the ability of television programming to teach elementary-school reading and arithmetic has been decisively demonstrated by the *Electric Company* and *Square One TV;* and the ability of television programming to teach middle-school science has been decisively demonstrated by *Three-Two-One Contact.* All four series have had millions of viewers, adults as well as children—they were remarkably cost effective; all four have shown television's facility in educating while entertaining— they stayed light on didacticism; and all four have attracted learners without the benefit of credit, certification, or compulsion. Moreover, the Workshop has developed a variety of ancillary educative tools, including the *Sesame Street Magazine,* which appears monthly and is directed toward preschoolers and which carries a *Parent's Guide* that is intended to assist adults in the business of childrearing and familial education.

One might look similarly at the program of college-level courses developed during the 1980s by the Annenberg/ Corporation for Public Broadcasting Project. The offerings range from *American National Government* to *The Brain* to *College Algebra* to *French in Action.* Each course is accompanied by a study guide. In 1988 alone more than 700 colleges were offering the courses to an audience of some 7.5 million viewers; between 1984 and 1988 over 100,000 of the viewers earned college credit through the Project's materials. One might look too at series addressed to more general audiences, series as diverse as *The Open Mind, Nova, Connections, The Body in Question, Nature, America, National Geographic Explorer,* and *The Long Search,* many of which have had study guides prepared for them through which viewers can go from the program content to books, articles, and other related print materials.

Beyond all this, it is well to bear in mind that the telecommunications industry is in the throes of a new revolution. Cable systems are now bringing scores of channels into the home, including in some communities channels permitting responsive and interactive television; disks and tapes are making possible the viewing of programs on demand; new forms of antennae receive signals bounced off satellites without the intervention of cable or broadcast systems; and the linkage of telecommunications and microcomputers is making available unprecedented sources of information for the home. Whatever else can be said about these new technologies, they are surely providing incomparable opportunities for teaching and learning that completely bypass schools and colleges and go directly into the household.

As for changes in the nature of work, it is a commonplace to note that the United States is in the midst of a transition from an industrial to a service and information economy and that this shift is affecting every aspect of American life.

In 1920 the number of persons engaged in manufacturing in the United States for the first time exceeded the number engaged in agriculture; in 1956 the number of persons doing white-collar work first exceeded the number doing blue-collar work. During the early 1960s, the economist Fritz Machlup began to talk about a "knowledge economy"; a few years later the sociologist Daniel Bell began to talk about a "post-industrial society"; and, contemporarily, Japanese telecommunications officials began to talk about an "information society." Today roughly half the American work force is occupied with what might be called the processing of knowledge—a phrase that would include people involved in education, entertainment, science, and culture, and who draw upon materials as different as musical tapes, industrial and commercial computer programs, and scientific data bases.[6]

We have tended in recent years to identify the skills people need successfully to negotiate an information society with the skills taught in the academic curricula of schools and colleges, and in some measure that is undeniably true—one must be able to read and write and calculate, in effect, one must have the elementary skills of communication, to deal with information. But the identification is at best limited. For one thing, as Richard Murnane has pointed out, we know less than we need to know about the so-called fit between schooling and the needs of the American economy. For another, there is increasing evidence that the more advanced information industries are going to have to develop their own internal educative agencies and operations to teach the knowledge and skills required by their work forces. When Nell P. Eurich undertook her study of education programs in American business corporations during the early 1980s, she discovered a sixty-billion dollar operation that extended from the elementary training programs of lines people of the Bell telephone system to the complex training programs associated with the research activities of IBM, Texas Instruments, and Wang Computing. Indeed, Wang ultimately joined with Digital Equipment, Data General, Raytheon, Honeywell, and other companies to establish the Wang Institute, which is empowered by the Commonwealth of Massachusetts to grant graduate degrees. Eurich further discovered that the manufacturers of the most complex information technology were the firms that maintained the most advanced education and training facilities—and in close collaboration with their research, development, and manufacturing operations. Her discoveries would seem to be emblematic of the future development of education in the American workplace.[7]

II

My argument has been that profound changes since World War II in the rearing of children and sweeping changes in the nature, uses, and delivery of information have radically transformed the ecology of education in the United States and fundamentally altered the circumstances within which schools and colleges carry on their work. Put otherwise, changes in the education proffered by families, day care centers, peer groups, television broadcasters, and workplaces have drastically altered the overall education being offered to the American people. The result has been a cacophony of teaching, the effects of which have been at best difficult to determine and even more difficult to assess.

This is not the place to review the research on teaching and learning in families, day care centers, and workplaces as well as through television, though it might be well to take a moment to lay aside some of the myths that have prevailed in traditional discourse about education. First, it is clear that the longstanding notion that the same teaching always has the same or similar effects on all learners is simply not true. We know that each sibling in the same household experiences what is for all intents and purposes a different family and hence a different familial education, and further, that although birth order has long been assumed to be the major variable it actually accounts for very little of the difference as compared with factors such as parental treatment, sibling interaction, and networks of kin and peers beyond the household. Similarly, we know that the same message conveyed by a popular medium of communication, whether through print or electronics, can be received quite variously by different individuals, depending on the background of the individual and the context in which the message is received. To cite but one example, Elihu Katz and Tamar Liebes found in research done at the Hebrew University of Jerusalem that the same episodes of the television serial *Dallas* were perceived quite differently by Russian-born Israeli immigrants, North-African Israeli immigrants, native-born Israeli Arabs, and native-born Israeli kibbutzniks. We also know from the work of Erik Erikson, James Coleman, Kenneth Keniston, and others that parents share their children with peer groups, particularly during adolescence. These peer groups serve a critical function in enabling boys and girls during the transition from childhood to adulthood to rehearse alternative ideas, values, and roles with other boys and girls filled with similar uncertainty. In effect, the adolescent peer group becomes another context for interpreting messages from the external world.[8]

Second, it is clear that the common notion that teaching is unidirectional from parent to child, from instructor to pupil, from expert to novice is at best simplistic. The human relationships involved in education are always bidirectional, and both the substance and the methods of teaching are continually transformed in the interaction that results. The so-called infant studies of the 1970s demonstrated the extent to which the behavior of the child inevitably affected the entire nurturing behavior of the parent. The school ethnographies of the 1970s and 1980s, with their emphasis on "negotiated contracts," pointed to the ways in which teachers and students reached agreements on how classes would be conducted and what each group would expect of the other. And we have known for a half century at least that workers set their own pace of work, and they surely do so in training programs as well as on the assembly line.[9]

Third, the social structure of the teaching situation is not in and of itself decisive with respect to the character of what is taught and learned. Single-parent families can nurture children in ways that aid and abet their academic achievement in schools; two-parent families can nurture children in ways that hinder and obstruct it. While home care of children by caretakers who are not kin is generally less educationally stimulating than institutional day care, an engaged and engaging caretaker in the home can provide educational stimulation of higher quality than a team of unengaged and unengaging caretakers in an institutional setting.[10]

Fourth, the influence of any particular educative institution is rarely direct and unalloyed; it is almost always mediated—that is, reflected, refracted, and interpreted—by other educative institutions. The family is probably the most important of these mediating agencies. Jennifer W. Bryce has documented the extent to which television education, from advertisements to soap operas, is commonly mediated by family discussions; Deborah Parr Benton has noted the same phenomenon with respect to museum education. Benjamin Bloom has pointed to the crucial role of families in the education and training of talented pianists, mathematicians, and athletes. From a quite different perspective, the school then takes its turn in mediating this familial education as it relates to television viewing, museum going, and training to be a pianist, a mathematician, or an athlete.[11]

Fifth, neither the processes of teaching and learning in these various educative institutions nor the character and significance of what is learned are all of a piece. The essence of a good deal of familial education is informal tuition, modeling, explaining, and correcting. The essence of most school education is systematic instruction. The forms of television education range from the subtle and not-so-subtle bombardment of commercials to the more dramatic and comprehensive instruction of documentaries. The forms of education in the workplace range from pure imitation as an apprentice to informal training as an understudy to formal instruction in a classroom. And, by every measure we have, the learning that results from these processes is exceedingly various. Robert Dreeben and Sara Lawrence Lightfoot have explicated the differences between what is taught and learned in families and what is taught and learned in schools, even when parents and schoolteachers are dealing with similar issues. Laurene Meringoff and her colleagues have explicated the differences between what children learn from a story read from a book and what they learn from that same story presented in an animated film on television with a voice-over of a text of the book (the children who experience the story over television remember much less of the story on their own and are less able to make inferences that draw on their own personal experience). Jean Lave and her colleagues have studied the arithmetic decision-making processes of adult shoppers in supermarkets in Orange County, California, discovering that shoppers whose computations were virtually error-free in the stores made frequent errors in parallel problems in a formal testing situation. (The shoppers averaged a startling 98 percent of error-free decision-making in the supermarkets as compared with a lackluster 59 percent on the formal tests.) And Lauren Resnick, reviewing the differences between cognitive learning in school and nonschool settings, has concluded that the dominant form of school learning is individual and involves "pure thought," symbol manipulation, and generalized theoretical principles, whereas the dominant form of nonschool learning is shared and involves tool manipulation, contextualized reasoning, and situation-specific competencies.[12]

Sixth, it is important to note that any one of the many institutions that educate can be the decisive influence in the life of any particular individual, depending upon personality, circumstance, and luck. To choose but a few examples from the educational biographies I included in *American Education: The Metropolitan Experience,* Elizabeth Dodge Huntington Clark obtained her most important education within the confines of her family and the YWCA; Morris Raphael Cohen received the decisive elements of his education in the cultural organizations of New York's Lower East Side and at the College of the City of New York and then Harvard; Arthur Flegenheimer, who had a fabulously successful career as a beer racketeer during the 1930s under the name Dutch Schultz, was profoundly influenced by what he learned in the Bergen Social Club, which served as the headquarters of a South Bronx street gang (his mother, Emma Flegenheimer, must have had a keen awareness of the Pinocchio Effect); William Santora, a factory worker, had his most important education in the United Electrical Workers Union and in the Communist party; while the black artist Jacob Lawrence had the decisive elements of his education in the Harlem Community Art Center and in the Schomburg Collection of African-American materials of the New York Public Library. I cite these instances because they make so clear the immense diversity in the sources and sites of the education that ultimately makes a difference in people's lives.[13]

Seventh, everything that needs to be learned does not necessarily have to be taught or taught in a particular place in a particular sequence at a particular time. As Robert McClintock has argued, there remain places for study in a world of instruction, places where individuals young and old can strike out on their own through reading, television viewing, computer programs, discussion groups, museum visits, attendance at lectures, or club activities to learn whatever they would like to learn, at their own pace and in their own way. I am profoundly impressed with the fact that in 1987, three quarters of a million people took the General Educational Development Tests, of whom 470,000 earned a high school equivalency credential. Roughly half of those took formal courses, but almost a third prepared independently according to their own educative and learning styles.[14]

Finally, there is a considerable difference between academic knowledge and everyday knowledge, between the knowledge taught and valued in school and the knowledge needed and valued in everyday life. Academic knowledge is a selection and an abstraction from everyday experience; it relates to that experience more or less but is far from identical with that experience. There is a politics that governs the selection and authentication of academic knowledge, and there are traditions that enshrine that knowledge in school and college curricula. Further, the business of mastering academic knowledge calls up a narrower range of intelligences than what is needed to master everyday knowledge. That thousands of individuals studying in nonschool settings can pass a series of school equivalency examinations is testimony to their brightness and determination, for they have been asked to demonstrate at most only a portion of what they have learned and to demonstrate it on a sampling of problems skewed in particular directions. The living of life itself would be a better indication of what they have ultimately mastered.[15]

III

There have been numerous policy recommendations during the 1970s and 1980s in the domains of child care, television broadcasting, and workplace training, but they have tended to deal with problems piecemeal and without relation to one another. The question that faces us now is whether it is possible to craft a set of policy recommendations that deals with education more comprehensively and that links the various parts of the education system more effectively.

Child care policy became an explicit matter of national concern at least twice before 1945—first, during the 1930s, as an element in the federal relief program of the New Deal, and then during the 1940s, as part of the federal effort to meet the needs of civilian war workers, especially women. It emerged again during the 1960s as an element in the congeries of programs known as the War on Poverty. Head Start, the single most popular creation of the community action effort established under the Economic Opportunity Act of 1964, was a comprehensive program of child development directed to four- and five-year-olds from low-income homes—it concerned itself with mental and physical health, child welfare and recreation, and intellectual development. A half million children were initially enrolled during the summer of 1965, and from 1966 to 1970 between 200,000 and 300,000 were enrolled annually in full-year programs with large numbers of additional children joining during the summers. Parents were involved from the beginning, as were child development professionals and paraprofessionals, and local political authorities were delighted with the grass-roots support the program generated. Without question, the youngsters clearly profited. For a time, a 1969 evaluation by the Westinghouse Corporation cast doubt upon the enterprise, with findings that the benefits of Head Start were proving ephemeral as the children proceeded into the elementary grades. But later studies, particularly those carried out during the 1970s and 1980s by David Weikart and his colleagues at the High/Scope Educational Research Foundation in Ypsilanti, Michigan, found significant and durable results, not only with respect to success in later schooling but also with regard to the ability to obtain and hold employment during early adulthood.[16]

Encouraged by the enthusiasm for the program, a coalition of child development experts, civil rights activists, feminists, church workers, and child advocates pushed the legislation known as the Comprehensive Child Development Act of 1971 through both houses of Congress. The legislation authorized a broad range of health, education, and welfare services for all children whose parents desired them and provided federal funds that enabled local communities to make decisions regarding their own priorities. Parents were to play decisive roles in the planning, administration, and operation of the programs, and the requirements of economically disadvantaged and handicapped children were to be given precedence. President Richard M. Nixon vetoed the bill, contending that the need for such a program of child development had not been demonstrated and that "for the federal government to plunge headlong financially into supporting child development would commit the vast moral authority of the national government to the side of communal approaches to child rearing over against the family-centered approach."[17]

Child care policy remained on the national agenda during the 1970s and 1980s, but opposition to a federal program increased, particularly from more conservative economic and religious interests. The coalition of 1971 seemed to fragment around differences of opinion concerning where child care services ought to be made available, where the services ought to be delivered and who ought to receive them, and who ought to control and carry out the programs. Senator Walter Mondale and Congressman John Brademas introduced child development legislation into both houses of Congress in 1973, but to no avail, and a series of White House Conferences on the Family during the Carter administration merely testified to the fragmentation of child advocacy interests.

The most ambitious set of policy formulations during the 1970s came from the Carnegie Council on Children, created by the Carnegie Corporation of New York. Prepared under the leadership of Kenneth Keniston, the commission's report of 1977, published under the title *All Our Children: The American Family Under Pressure,* recommended a multibillion dollar federal program of income maintenance, job creation, and health, welfare, and educational services—a package that, though its several elements had been under discussion for many years, seemed too ambitious and costly at the time to receive serious consideration in legislative circles. A decade later, in 1988, new programs of child care were finally legislated by Congress, but only as subsidiary elements in the welfare reform effort led by Senator Daniel Patrick Moynihan and Congressman Thomas J. Downey. And that same year, as evidence of what still remained to be done, the Children's Defense Fund provided the startling fact that almost a quarter century after Head Start had been inaugurated, fewer than 20 percent of the 2.4 million children living in poverty who were eligible for Head Start and whose parents wished them to participate in it were being served by the program.[18]

Television policy has been confused in recent years by the rapid and radical changes in telecommunications and computing technology, by the vigorous legal debate over whether television broadcasting should be covered by the provisions of the First Amendment to the United States Constitution, by the multiplication of cable television systems throughout the nation, and by the extraordinary internationalizing of electronic information exchange during the 1970s and 1980s. Despite these trends, the most significant drift of television policy during the 1970s and 1980s was toward deregulation on the part of the Federal Communications Commission. Even so, the recommendations of three policy documents of the 1970s, none of which was taken seriously in its own time or since, remain interesting and worthy of consideration. I refer to Robert Blakely's *The People's Instrument: A Philosophy of Programming for Public Television* (1971), a report sponsored by the Charles F. Kettering Foundation; William Melody's *Children's Television: The Economics of Exploitation* (1973), a report sponsored by the John and Mary R. Markle Foundation on behalf of Action for Children's Television, and *A Public Trust: The Report of the Carnegie Commission on the Future of Public Broadcasting* (1979), a report sponsored by the Carnegie Corporation of New York.

Blakely's statement of program goals for public broadcasting is broad and comprehensive and shows a firm grasp of the potential educational function of present-day radio and television broadcasting. He speaks of the need of public television to entertain as well as instruct; to provide an open forum for debate, discussion, and participation in the making of public decisions; to perform a variety of public services, from providing information about employment opportunities to carrying reports of government proceedings; to help Americans cultivate the critical ability to use, and not be used by, the media of popular communication; and to complement and expand the educational opportunities provided by schools and colleges. Most important, Blakely's is not a narrow elitist agenda for giving the public what he thinks it "ought to want"; it is an agenda that takes full account of the need for public broadcasting to serve what Herbert Gans has referred to as a variety of "taste cultures."[19]

Melody's study traces the decline in the extent, variety, and quality of children's television programming during the 1960s and 1970s as commercial interests came to view children as a special market for special products, the advertisements for which were surrounded by televised versions of comic books. And he joins the sorry history of that decline to the prediction that economic factors will cause the situation to worsen—a prediction that has since been more than confirmed by events. As a remedy for the situation, he puts forward a proposal that the FCC remove children's television from the commercial market and seek alternative financing for programs addressed to the general needs and interests of children in the form of institutional advertising, private underwriting, and government subsidies. The study was submitted to the FCC in January 1973 as part of testimony at the commission's hearings on children's television. Needless to say, the commission, much in a deregulatory mood, took no action on the proposals. In fact, subsequent efforts to stem the decline Melody forecasted faced growing resistance in the commission and the Congress and, during the Reagan administrations, presidential vetoes.[20]

A Public Trust was an effort to respond to the politicization of the Corporation for Public Broadcasting during the 1970s. It proposed that the corporation be replaced by a Public Telecommunications Trust with a "highly insulated, semiautonomous division" called the Program Services Endowment that would have the "sole objective of supporting creative excellence," and that the federal contribution rise to $600 million annually by 1985. The report had little effect on President Jimmy Carter or the Congress; no legislation was introduced or enacted, and the level of support the commission urged was not forthcoming. But, again, the commission's argument for a reasonably financed federal authority that could be insulated from narrow political whim and that could devote its efforts to supporting a rich variety of programming along the lines supported by Robert Blakely remained on the public agenda for consideration.[21]

There has been too little attention in the policy literature of the past two decades to issues concerning education in the workplace. When Nell Eurich undertook her study for the Carnegie Foundation for the Advancement of Teaching that became *Corporate Classrooms* in 1985, she was astonished, first, by how few studies had been done prior to her own, second, by how little knowledge companies like IBM or Bell Telephone seemed to have of the scope, cost, or character of the education programs they were conducting, and, third, by how little thought had been given to possible national policies in that domain. She cited the suggestions of James Botkin and his associates in 1982 that a Presidential Commission on Technology and Productivity be created and that a new High Technology Morrill Act be passed to do for present-day postindustrial development what the original Morrill Act had done to assist agricultural and industrial development. And she herself recommended the creation of a Strategic Council for Educational Development that would assess the nation's emerging needs for education and training, identify the available resources for meeting those needs, and recommend policies to coordinate and facilitate the effort.[22]

Two years after Eurich's report appeared, the Educational Testing Service published a report by Richard Venezky, Carl Kaestle, and Andrew Sum entitled *The Subtle Danger: Reflections on the Literacy Abilities of America's Young Adults,* which sought to develop policies for dealing with the limited literacy skills of young people between the ages of twenty-one and twenty-five that had been revealed in a 1986 study carried out under the National Assessment of Educational Progress. One of the most important recommendations of that report was that employers recognize the obligation of workplaces to develop the literacy proficiency of existing employees, particularly the ability to read in complex and thoughtful ways. Beginning with literacy, of course, one might imagine many other proficiencies that adults might realize they need but did not learn when they were children—a range of skills from civic competence to foreign language proficiency to parenting, particularly if there is a child care center in the workplace for the children of employees.[23]

In addition to these recommendations for more or less formal education programs, there is the more general recommendation that has been in the policy literature since at least the 1973 HEW task force report entitled *Work in America*—namely, that work be organized in such a way that it presents continuous opportunities for the kind of learning that enables workers to perform tasks with ever wider vision, ever increasing competence, and an ever greater sense of the value of their labor in the larger scheme of things. This can be done in myriad ways, from worker participation in decision making to the redesign of jobs and the reallocation of authority and responsibility for the definition of jobs. Interestingly, such efforts almost always lead to improved productivity. Further, they provide invaluable training in the general competencies associated with democratic participation in the affairs of the society at large. Indeed, there may be few more significant opportunities in the larger educative apparatus of the American community for the learning of such skills.[24]

It remains to consider the relation of school and college policies to these policies concerning other institutions in which education occurs. It goes without saying that schools and colleges occupy a special place in the configuration of modern American education. Their primary role is to provide opportunities for systematic study and instruction, while for many other institutions the provision of education is a subsidiary role. What is more, schools and colleges are currently more subject to public policy than, say, families or television or workplaces, though we should be aware that that is not necessarily the case in many other countries, nonsocialist as well as socialist. Finally, schools and colleges provide an intensive educative experience that consumes much of the time of children, adolescents, and many young adults over extended periods of their lives. That said, we also need to recognize that schools and colleges cannot accomplish the educative tasks of a modern civilization on their own, if indeed they ever could. The assumption that they can and should accomplish those tasks by themselves has been one of the prime failings of the policy literature of the 1980s, beginning with *A Nation at Risk*. Given the insights that are flowing from the recent research on situated learning and cognition in context, given what we know about the power and pervasiveness of the other educators, given the extent to which the effectiveness of schooling is dependent upon and vulnerable to the influence of the other educators (especially the family and television), and given what we must accept about the discontent with schooling on the part of significant segments of the American community, the assumption is simply untenable. A much broader view of education is demanded, one that sees schools and colleges as crucially important but not solely responsible.

In this respect, the school and college policy literature of the 1970s again holds the clue to a more comprehensive approach, for that literature granted from the outset that formal institutions of education need to work in concert with families, civic agencies, telecommunications facilities, cultural institutions, and workplaces if their programs are to be realistic as well as academically respectable. It even urged the schools and colleges to "broker" and "negotiate" educational opportunities for students in such organizations. Only in a thoughtfully planned collaboration can schools and colleges carry on well their nurturance of intellectual, social, and emotional competence. Schools, in the very nature of their work, depend especially upon families, however varied the structures families assume within the different kinship systems of the American population. Indeed, I believe it is the extraordinarily diverse education families have provided during the 1970s and 1980s and the conjunctions and disjunctions between that education and the education schools have sought to provide that have created some of the most difficult problems of schooling in our time. Schools and colleges also need to be aware of what is taught and mistaught over television, in part so they can seize opportunities to enhance their own instruction and in part so they can challenge, counter, and correct what they perceive as error. In the end, only in a thoughtfully planned collaboration can the waste resulting from the cacophony of teaching be reduced and the opportunities for access and stimulus inherent in that cacophony be maximized.[25]

Three additional points need comment. First, in thinking more comprehensively about where education goes on and ought to go on in a modern postindustrial community, we need to focus much more sharply than we have in the past on the kinds of teaching and learning that different institutions foster most effectively and, additionally, on which students want and need to learn what, and when, where, how, and from whom they should learn it. Alison Clarke-Stewart has wisely maintained that parent education programs that really hope to make a difference in the quality of parental child care should probably begin with the parents' own active involvement with their children at home. John Goodlad has argued in several of his recent books that the schools are unusually well equipped to focus on cognitive development in such domains as literature, mathematics, science, social studies, and foreign languages, and, more generally, to sharpen the skills of critical thinking, and that if young people miss certain instruction in those domains in school they are not likely to receive that instruction elsewhere. And Jean Lave and Sylvia Scribner have indicated that certain specific skills associated with the production and distribution of goods and services are best learned in the particular conditions of the workplace. Furthermore, Benjamin Bloom has argued that, while extraordinary talent in music or athletics is frequently given its initial development in the household, there comes a time when instruction outside the household with a special teacher is vital for continuing progress. Goodlad has lamented the amount of time young people spend in school learning the sorts of social skills they would learn quite satisfactorily in other institutional contexts. And Joan Stark, Malcolm Lowther, and Donald Schön, in arguing for a clearer integration between liberal and professional studies, have also pointed to the need for colleges and workplaces, through internships, to achieve greater general integration between theory and practice if professional education, in which more than half the students in higher education are enrolled, is to be even minimally effective. The point is simply that certain institutions are better sites for particular forms of education than others.[26]

In addition, one must also bear in mind the perceptions and preferences of clienteles. Adolescent girls who have dropped out of school to bear children might be fascinated by classes in child health and nutrition at the same time that they would be repelled by classes in mathematics and foreign languages. During the 1970s, Peter L. Buttenwieser developed a public school in Philadelphia called the Durham Child Development Center on just that principle. He began with a crèche for the infants and parenting classes for the adolescent mothers and added new grades and subjects each year as the infants and mothers grew older. He also involved the grandparents so that, after four or five years, he was presiding over a three-generation facility that offered a wide range of instruction for interested preschoolers, adolescents, and adults—including, incidentally, some of the mathematics that had earlier been eschewed. Needless to say, the three generations also taught one another both inside and outside the school. The fact is that, even when bolstered by compulsory attendance requirements enforced by diligent attendance officers, schools cannot function effectively in communities where parents have no confidence in those schools and children have no interest in what they are attempting to teach. The money that sustains such institutions might occasionally be better spent in developing instructional programs of interest to the parents and their children in community institutions that do have their confidence—community health and nutrition centers, for example, or Police Athletic League and Boy's Club of America athletic programs.

Likewise, the possibilities of adolescent and adult education programs in connection with preparation for work or advancement in the workplace have never been fully exploited—one need only compare the well-organized apprentice training programs of countries like France and the Federal Republic of Germany with the more haphazard apprentice training in the United States under the former Comprehensive Employment and Training Act or the present Job Training Partnership Act to realize how differently countries respond to the same need. Recent research at the Conservation of Human Resources Project at Columbia University has pointed to the rapid changes in the structure and definition of jobs in the banking, insurance, and textile industries and the new kinds of abstract knowledge and interpersonal skills required by those who perform those jobs. But as has already been indicated, the tendency on the part of educational analysts is to leap to the conclusion that what is required is more systematic study of the sort best offered in school. That might indeed be true, but it might also be true that many of the cognitive and interpersonal skills would be better learned in the workplace by people who have become disenchanted with schools, or at least better learned in some combination of workplace and school.[27]

Second, given the multitude of educational opportunities and the changing character of educational needs over a lifetime, one of the most important things for individuals to learn early and well is how to obtain the education they would like to have at any given period of their lives. Many middle-class youngsters see the process modeled within the family as parents arrange a complex mosaic of music lessons, scouting opportunities, academic tutoring, ice-skating classes, and religious instruction for their children, and indeed as parents themselves participate in the seminars, workshops, institutes, and continuing education programs that mark the successive stages of present-day careers. Lower-class youngsters are less likely to see the process modeled, though their need to be aware of and to take advantage of educational opportunities that are available to them may be even greater. Information about such opportunities can be distributed through many sources, from public-access cable television channels to community health centers to local supermarkets. Given the present organization of education in the United States, however, I believe the process of actually seeking out and taking advantage of available educational opportunities ought to be systematically taught and modeled in schools and colleges. One might think of it as the nurturance of educational autonomy in students, an autonomy that will serve them well all the rest of their lives.

Third, for schools and colleges to be able to "broker" and "negotiate" the experiences of students in other educative milieus through cooperative arrangements with neighborhood organizations, cultural institutions, government agencies, television stations, and workplaces will require a very fundamental restructuring that makes the walls of the schools and colleges, so to speak, more permeable. There has been a good deal of discussion of school restructuring in recent years, in part by educators like Theodore R. Sizer, who would like to see much more power and prerogative in the hands of teachers, in part by advocates of various forms of administrative decentralization, who would like to see much more collaboration among principals, teachers, parents, and other local community representatives in the design and development of individual school programs. Such goals have much to commend them, but they are in the end insufficient; for the restructuring that will make possible fruitful collaboration among all the institutions involved in education across the entire lifespan is much more fundamental and in many ways even more difficult to achieve. It involves collaboration among many public and private agencies run by many different kinds of professionals, most of whom are not in the habit of sharing budgets, facilities, and clienteles. And it involves community leadership of the sort that has not been widely manifest in recent years. Yet only such a fundamental restructuring will bring together the educational opportunities Americans require during the last years of the twentieth century.[28]

There is a final point to be made about cacophony, namely, that cacophony may be noisy and confusing, and we may need to reduce it at some points in order to enhance the effectiveness of education, but that it also has certain essential virtues. The late John Herman Randall, Jr., who for years professed the history of philosophy at Columbia University, used to teach Plato's *Republic* as an anti-utopia, his argument being that Plato wanted to frighten readers into recognizing the totalitarian monstrosity that resulted from the drive to make the entire teaching of a society consonant. There are important opportunities in cacophony, particularly opportunities for examining alternatives in values, ideas, and aspirations and for choosing among them; those opportunities for examining and choosing are essential in any education that befits a free people. They must not be lost in the effort to enhance efficiency.

NOTES

1. James A. Sweet and Larry L. Bumpass, *American Families and Households* (New York: Russell Sage Foundation, 1987), 349, 177–178, 264, 148–149; and Suzanne M. Bianchi and Daphne Spain, *American Women in Transition* (New York: Russell Sage Foundation, 1986), 225–230.

2. Hope Jensen Leichter, "Some Perspectives on the Family as Educator," in Hope Jensen Leichter, ed., *The Family as Educator* (New York: Teachers College Press, 1974), 1–43, and "The Concept of Educative Style," *Teachers College Record*, 75 (December 1973):239–250.

3. Robert S. Lynd and Helen Merrell Lynd, *Middletown: A Study in American Culture* (New York: Harcourt, Brace, 1929), 135, 143–144, and *Middletown in Transition: A Study in Cultural Conflicts* (New York: Harcourt, Brace, 1937), 170–172; and Theodore Caplow et al., *Middletown Families: Fifty Years of Change and Continuity* (Minneapolis: University of Minnesota Press, 1982), 22–25.

4. Bianchi and Spain, *American Women in Transition*, 225–230.

5. "Black Churches: Can They Strengthen the Black Family?" *Carnegie Quarterly*, 33 (Fall/Winter 1987–1988):1–7; and "Black Churches: New Mission on Family," *New York Times*, August 24, 1988, A1, A18.

6. Fritz Machlup, *The Production and Distribution of Knowledge in the United States* (Princeton: Princeton University Press, 1962); Daniel Bell, *The Coming of Post-Industrial Society: A Venture in Social Forecasting* (New York: Basic Books, 1973); and Anthony Smith, "Telecommunications and the Fading of the Industrial Age: Information and the Post-Industrial Economy," in James Curran, Anthony Smith, and Pauline Wingate, eds., *Impacts and Influences: Essays on Media Power in the Twentieth Century* (London: Methuen, 1987), 331–337.

7. Richard J. Murnane, "Education and the Productivity of the Work Force: Looking Ahead," in Robert E. Litan, Robert Z. Lawrence, and Charles L. Schultze, eds., *American Living Standards: Threats and Challenges* (Washington, D. C.: The Brookings Institute, 1988), 215–245; Nell P. Eurich, *Corporate Classrooms: The Learning Business* (Princeton, N. J.: The Carnegie Foundation for the Advancement of Teaching, 1985); and Bonita L. Betters-Reed, "A History and Analysis of Three Innovative Graduate Institutions: The Arthur D. Little Management Education Institute, The Massachusetts General Hospital Institute of Health Professions, and the Wang Institute of Graduate Studies" (doctoral thesis, Boston College, 1982).

8. David C. Rowe and Robert Plomin, "The Importance of Nonshared (E_1) Environmental Influences in Behavioral Development," *Developmental Psychology*, 17 (September 1981):517–531; Robert Plomin and Denise Daniels, "Why Are Children in the Same Family So Different from One Another?" *Behavioral and Brain Sciences*, 10 (November 1987):1–60; Elihu Katz and Tamar Liebes, "Mutual Aid in the Decoding of *Dallas:* Preliminary Notes from a Cross-Cultural Study," in Phillip Drummond and Richard Paterson, *Television in Transition: Papers from the First International Television Studies Conference* (London: British Film Institute, 1985), 187–198; Erik H. Erikson, *Childhood and Society* (New York: Norton, 1950); James S. Coleman, *The Adolescent Society: The Social Life of the Teenager and Its Impact on Education* (New York: Free Press, 1961); Kenneth Keniston, *The Uncommitted: Alienated Youth in American Society* (New York: Harcourt, Brace, 1965); Vivian Center Seltzer, *Adolescent Social Develop-*

ment: Dynamic Functional Interaction (Lexington, Mass.: Lexington Books, 1982); and Francis A. J. Ianni, *The Search for Structure: A Report on American Youth Today* (New York: Free Press, 1989).

9. Richard Q. Bell, "A Reinterpretation of the Direction of Effects in Studies of Socialization," *Psychological Review*, 75 (March 1968):81–95; Kenneth Kaye, "Infants' Effects upon Their Mothers' Teaching Strategies," in John C. Glidewell, ed., *The Social Context of Learning and Development* (New York: Gardner Press, 1977), 173–206; Mary Haywood Metz, *Classrooms and Corridors: The Crisis of Authority in Desegregated Secondary Schools* (Berkeley: University of California Press, 1978); Vito Perrone et al., *Portraits of High Schools* (Princeton, N. J.: Carnegie Foundation for the Advancement of Teaching, 1985); Arthur G. Powell, Eleanor Farrar, and David K. Cohen, *The Shopping Mall High School: Winners and Losers in the Educational Marketplace* (Boston: Houghton Mifflin, 1985); and F. J. Roethlisberger, *Management and Morale* (Cambridge, Mass.: Harvard University Press, 1941), 22–26.

10. Reginald M. Clark, *Family Life and School Achievement: Why Poor Black Children Succeed or Fail* (Chicago: University of Chicago Press, 1983); and Alison Clarke-Stewart, *Child Care in the Family: A Review of Research and Some Propositions for Policy* (New York: Academic Press, 1977), 85–115.

11. Hope Jensen Leichter, "Families and Communities as Educators: Some Concepts of Relationship," in Leichter, ed., *Families and Communities as Educators* (New York: Teachers College Press, 1979), 32–40; Hope Jensen Leichter et al., "Family Contexts of Television," *Educational Communication and Television Journal*, 33 (Spring 1985): 26–40; Jennifer W. Bryce, "Families and Television: An Ethnographic Approach" (doctoral thesis, Teachers College, Columbia University, 1980); Jennifer W. Bryce and Hope Jensen Leichter, "The Family and Television: Forms of Mediation," *Journal of Family Issues*, 4 (June 1983): 309–328; Deborah Parr Benton, "Intergenerational Interaction in Museums" (doctoral thesis, Teachers College, Columbia University, 1979); and Benjamin S. Bloom, ed., *Developing Talent in Young People* (New York: Ballantine, 1985).

12. Hope Jensen Leichter, "Some Perspectives on the Family as Educator," and "Families and Communities as Educators"; Vito Perrone et al. *Portraits of High Schools;* Robert Dreeben, *On What Is Learned in School* (Reading, Mass.: Addison-Wesley, 1968); Sara Lawrence Lightfoot, *Worlds Apart: Relationships Between Families and Schools* (New York: Basic Books, 1978); Laurene K. Meringoff, "The Influence of the Medium on Children's Story Apprehension," *Journal of Educational Psychology*, 72 (April 1980): 240–249; Laurene K. Meringoff et al., "How Is Children's Learning from Television Distinctive? Exploiting the Medium Methodologically," in Jennings Bryant and Daniel R. Anderson, *Children's Understanding of Television: Research on Attention and Comprehension* (New York: Academic Press, 1983), chap. 6; Jean Lave, Michael Murtaugh, and Olivia de la Rocha, "The Dialectic of Arithmetic in Grocery Shopping," in Barbara Rogoff and Jean Lave, eds., *Everyday Cognition: Its Development in Social Context* (Cambridge, Mass.: Harvard University Press, 1984), 67–94; and Lauren B. Resnick, "Learning in School and Out," *Educational Researcher*, 16 (December 1987): 13–20.

13. Lawrence A. Cremin, *American Education: The Metropolitan Experience, 1876–1980* (New York: Harper & Row, 1988), chap. 13.

14. Robert McClintock, "Toward a Place for Study in a World of Instruction," *Teachers College Record*, 73 (December 1971):161–205; American Council on Education, General Educational Development Testing Service, *The 1987*

GED Statistical Report (Washington, D. C.: American Council on Education, 1988); and Andrew G. Malizio and Douglas R. Whitney, *Who Takes the GED Tests? A National Study of Spring 1980 Examinees* (Washington, D.C.: American Council on Education, 1981). The statistics on preparation for the 1987 GED tests were provided by the staff of the General Educational Development Testing Service of the American Council on Education.

15. There is a considerable literature, emanating from disciplines as different as anthropology, sociology, psychology, linguistics, and history, on academic knowledge vis-à-vis everyday knowledge, including Milton Singer, *When a Great Tradition Modernizes: An Anthropological Approach to Indian Civilization* (New York: Praeger, 1972); Pierre Bourdieu and Jean-Claude Passeron, *The Inheritors: French Students and Their Relation to Culture,* translated by Richard Nice (Chicago: University of Chicago Press, 1979); David R. Olson, Nancy Torrance, and Angela Hildyard, *Literacy, Language, and Learning: The Nature and Consequences of Reading and Writing* (New York: Cambridge University Press, 1985); and Ellen Condliffe Lagemann, *The Politics of Knowledge: The Carnegie Corporation, Philanthropy, and Public Policy* (Middletown: Wesleyan University Press, 1989).

16. Edward Zigler and Jeanette Valentine, eds., *Project Head Start: A Legacy of the War on Poverty* (New York: Free Press, 1979); *The Impact of Head Start: An Evaluation of the Effects of Head Start on Children's Cognitive and Affective Development* (Westinghouse Learning Corporation/Ohio University, June 12, 1969); D. P. Weikart et al., "Longitudinal Results of the Ypsilanti Perry Preschool Project," *Monographs of the High/Scope Educational Research Foundation,* 1970, no. 1; and L. J. Schweinhart and D. P. Weikart, "Young Children Grow Up: The Effects of the Perry Preschool Program on Youths Through Age Fifteen," ibid., 1980, no. 7.

17. Gilbert Y. Steiner, *The Children's Cause* (Washington D.C.: The Brookings Institution, 1976), chap. 5; and *Congressional Record* (daily ed.), December 10, 1971, S46059.

18. Kenneth Keniston et al., *All Our Children: The American Family Under Pressure* (New York: Harcourt Brace Jovanovich, 1977); Children's Defense Fund, *A Call for Action to Make Our Nation Safe for Children: A Briefing Book on the Status of American Children in 1988* (Washington, D.C.: Children's Defense Fund, 1988). For a review of the social and political context of issues of child care, see also Alfred J. Kahn and Sheila B. Kamerman, *Child Care: Facing the Hard Choices,* (Dover, Mass.: Auburn House, 1987).

19. Robert J. Blakely, *The People's Instrument: A Philosophy of Programming for Public Television* (Washington, D.C.: Public Affairs Press, 1971); and Herbert J. Gans, *Popular Culture and High Culture: An Analysis and Evaluation of Taste* (New York: Basic Books, 1974).

20. William Melody, *Children's Television: The Economics of Exploitation* (New Haven: Yale University Press, 1973). For a more recent assessment of the state of children's television, see Edward L. Palmer, *Television and America's Children: A Crisis of Neglect* (New York: Oxford University Press, 1988), which, interestingly, sets the American situation within an international context.

21. *A Public Trust: The Report of the Carnegie Commission on the Future of Public Broadcasting* (New York: Bantam, 1979), 14.

22. Eurich, *Corporate Classrooms.*

23. Richard L. Venezky, Carl F. Kaestle, and Andrew M. Sum, *The Subtle Danger: Reflections on the Literacy Abilities of America's Young Adults* (Princeton, N.J.: Educational Testing Service, 1987).

24. *Work in America: Report of a Special Task Force to the Secretary of Health, Education, and Welfare* (Cambridge, Mass.: The MIT Press, 1973); James O'-Toole, *Work, Learning, and the American Future* (San Francisco: Jossey-Bass, 1977); and John Simmons and William Mares, *Working Together: Employee Participation in Action* (New York: Knopf, 1983). For the role of worker participation in decision making in furthering the general competences associated with democratic participation in the affairs of the society at large, see Carole Pateman, *Participation and Democratic Theory* (Cambridge: Cambridge University Press, 1970).

25. The theme of institutional collaboration that ran through the policy literature of the 1970s was sounded again in a small number of the education reports of the 1980s, including *Barriers to Excellence: Our Children at Risk* (Boston: National Coalition of Advocates for Students, 1985), *Children in Need: Investment Strategies for the Educationally Disadvantaged* (New York: Committee for Economic Development, 1987), *The Forgotten Half: Pathways to Success for America's Youth and Young Families* (Washington, D.C.: Youth and America's Future: The William T. Grant Commission on Work, Family, and Citizenship, 1988), *Turning Points: Preparing American Youth for the 21st Century* (Washington, D.C.: Carnegie Council on Adolescent Development, 1989), and *Investing in People: A Strategy to Address America's Workforce Crisis* (Washington, D.C.: GPO, 1989). One further point needs to be made about efforts at institutional collaboration, often referred to as partnerships. They commonly involve arrangements among public, nonprofit private, and profit-making organizations, and unless they are sustained by continuing public support they are not likely to prove durable. We have known at least since the 1840s that private wealth is too limited, too uncertain, too unevenly distributed, and too unresponsive to the public weal to serve as the economic foundation of a genuine system of popular education in the United States, whatever its particular structures at any given time. And we have learned since the 1950s that the federal government must bear an increasing measure of the cost of that system if equality of educational opportunity is truly to prevail. In the end, as Justice Holmes once remarked, the taxes that provide such public support are the cost of civilization.

26. Clarke-Stewart, *Child Care in the Family;* John I. Goodlad, *What Schools Are For* (Bloomington, Ind.: Phi Delta Kappa Educational Foundation, 1979), and *A Place Called School: Prospects for the Future* (New York: McGraw-Hill Book Company, 1984); Lave, Murtaugh, and de la Rocha, "The Dialectic of Arithmetic in Grocery Shopping," in Rogoff and Lave, eds., *Everyday Cognition,* 67–94; Sylvia Scribner, "Studying Working Intelligence," in ibid., 9–40; Bloom, ed., *Developing Talent in Young People;* Joan S. Stark and Malcolm A. Lowther, *Strengthening the Ties That Bind: Integrating Undergraduate Liberal and Professional Study* (Professional Preparation Project, School of Education, University of Michigan, 1988); and Donald A. Schön, *Educating the Reflective Practitioner: Toward a New Design for Teaching and Learning in the Professions* (San Francisco: Jossey-Bass, 1987).

27. Harold J. Noah and Max A. Eckstein, *International Study of Business/Industry Involvement with Education* (New York: The Institute of Philosophy and Politics of Education, Teachers College, Columbia University, Occasional

Paper Number 4, 1987); Stephen F. Hamilton, "Apprenticeship as a Transition to Adulthood in West Germany," *American Journal of Education*, 95 (February 1987):314–345; Sar A. Levitan and Frank Gallo, *A Second Chance: Training for Jobs* (Kalamazoo, Mich.: W. E. Upjohn Institute for Employment Research, 1988); Olivier Bertrand and Thierry Noyelle, *Human Resources and Corporate Strategy: Technological Change in Banks and Insurance Companies—France, Germany, Japan, Sweden, United States* (Paris: OECD, 1988); Thomas R. Bailey, "Education and the Transformation of Markets and Technology in the Textile Industry" (Technical Paper No. 2, National Center on Education and Employment, Teachers College, Columbia University, 1988); and *The Forgotten Half.* Having referred to the superior organization of the French and German apprenticeship training programs, I should also note that, insofar as those programs tend to stream young people into separate educational arrangements largely on the basis of social class background, they provide unsatisfactory models for American education. Americans will have to fashion a new model of school-workplace collaboration, equally well organized but more open, exploratory, and experimental on the part of the young people.

28. Theodore R. Sizer, *Horace's Compromise: The Dilemma of the American High School* (Boston: Houghton Mifflin, 1984); and AASA/NAESP/NASSP School-Based Management Task Force, *School-Based Management: A Strategy for Better Learning* (Arlington, Va.: AASA Publications, 1988). Recent programs of the Charles F. Kettering Foundation in Dayton, Ohio, and the UPS Foundation in Greenwich, Connecticut, have attempted to develop the community leadership and institutional collaboration that are needed to maximize the effectiveness of available educational resources.

EDUCATION
AS POLITICS

In America, as a matter of fact, education plays a different
and, politically, incomparably more important role than in
other countries. —HANNAH ARENDT,
"The Crisis in Education"

I

Education has always served political functions insofar as
it affects, or at least is believed and intended to affect, the
future character of the community and the state. Aristotle
explicated the relationship in the classic discussion of education he included in the *Politics.* Recall his argument there:
it is impossible to talk about education apart from some
conception of the good life; people will inevitably differ in
their conceptions of the good life, and hence they will inevitably disagree on matters of education; therefore the discussion of education falls squarely within the domain of
politics. In more recent times, commentators from Thomas
Jefferson to Horace Mann to John Dewey have applied
these Aristotelian doctrines to the American experience,
arguing the inescapable connection between education and
the character of the American polity.

For Jefferson, the goals of education were to diffuse
knowledge, inculcate virtue (including patriotism), and cultivate learning; he thought these ends would best be

achieved in public schools and colleges dedicated to preparing an informed citizenry and a humanely trained leadership. Once the schools and colleges had done their work, a free and responsible press would continue the education of the public in public affairs. Horace Mann accepted these Jeffersonian propositions but went beyond them to call for a common school that would receive children of all creeds, classes, and backgrounds (Jefferson made no provision for African-Americans in his proposals, while Mann stood mute on the matter of racial mixing in the schools, and neither had much to say about the education of women) and would seek to kindle in them a spirit of amity and mutual respect that the conflicts of adult life could never destroy. For Mann, the social responsibilities of the school in an increasingly heterogeneous society were every bit as crucial to the welfare of the republic as its intellectual responsibilities.

John Dewey made those social responsibilities even more extensive, more purposive, and more explicit. He cast the school as an instrument of reform that would not only prepare young people to make informed and independent judgments but also equip them to participate actively, with others, in the continued improvement of the large-scale industrial society that was coming into being. The ideal school, Dewey maintained, would be "an embryonic community life, active with types of occupations that reflect the life of the larger society, and permeated throughout with the spirit of art, history, and science." The task of the teacher would be to introduce children to that community life, saturating them with the spirit of service and providing them with the instruments of effective self-direction. When schools carried out that task, Dewey promised, Americans would have "the deepest and best guarantee of a larger society which is worthy, lovely, and harmonious." Thus did philosophical, social, and financial—they ranged from skepticism over the core curriculum to opposition to school rezoning. A number of "outside" organizations became interested in the controversies and sought to influence them—Allen Zoll's superpatriotic National Council for American Education was one; charges of communism, socialism, and un-Americanism were hurled, and in the end Goslin's position became untenable. James B. Conant reviewed Hulburd's book in the *New York Times Book Review*, cautioning readers against the smear techniques that had marked the discussion of school affairs in Pasadena and warning that the same sorts of controversy could easily engulf other communities; and magazines such as the *Saturday Evening Post* broadcast the story of Pasadena's problems to a nationwide audience. In the end, the Pasadena crisis dramatized the struggle between traditionalists and modernists in education and the related issues of political and religious conservatism and liberalism that swirled around that struggle during the late 1940s and early 1950s.[2]

The Little Rock crisis symbolized the struggles over school desegregation that followed in the wake of *Brown v. Board of Education* in 1954. The City of Little Rock, under the leadership of its elected school board and its superintendent, Virgil Blossom, prepared a plan in 1955 for the gradual integration of the public schools, beginning at the high school level in 1957 and moving successively to the junior high school and elementary school levels thereafter. That plan was mandated by the federal district court in 1956. As the school year was about to begin in September 1957, however, Governor Orville Faubus declared a state of emergency, called up the Arkansas National Guard, and ordered the guard to prevent the integration of Central High School in the interest of preserving public safety. The federal district court, in turn, instructed the National Guard

Dewey—and with him many of the Progressives—
the social responsibilities of the school and harness
ing more directly to particular social ends. In the p
education was politicized.[1]

That politicization, which became ever more a
during the twentieth century, deepened significantly
the years following World War II in all domains of
tion, but especially in the domain of schooling. The
were legion and often colored by local traditions,
they tended to cluster around disagreements over p
loyalty, religious orthodoxy, moral purity, and
quality. And with remarkable frequency they explod
"crises"—and that quite apart from the tendency
press to style any conflict over schooling involvin
than a dozen people a crisis. Four such crises wer
cially emblematic of the politicization of schooling
postwar era: the crisis over progressive educat
Pasadena, California, during the late 1940s and
1950s; the crisis over school desegregation in Little
Arkansas, during the late 1950s; the crisis over sch
centralization in New York City during the late 196
the crisis over moral and religious values in Ka
County, West Virginia, during the early 1970s.

The Pasadena crisis attracted nationwide attentior
in 1951 the journalist David Hulburd published *Th*
pened in Pasadena, recounting the story of Willard G
appointment as superintendent of schools in Pasad
1948, his initial efforts to introduce a number of pr
sive reforms into the Pasadena school curriculum ir
and 1949, the rise of opposition to these reforms ir
and 1950, and his resignation as superintendent in 1
the request of the same board that had appointed hi
years earlier. What becomes clear from the Hulburc
is that the issues that divided the citizens of Pasadena

to cease obstructing its order to integrate the school. The governor withdrew the guard; the black students who had been assigned to Central High School were admitted; and threats and violence immediately took over outside the school and occasionally inside as well. President Dwight Eisenhower then ordered federal troops to Arkansas to enforce the court's order and preserve the peace. The schools were kept open during the remainder of the 1957–58 academic year, and one black student was actually graduated in May. During the summer of 1958, Faubus was elected by a large majority to an unprecedented third term as governor; a defiant legislature passed a series of laws permitting the shutting down of public schools forced to integrate; and the Little Rock schools were closed. The first phase of the crisis ended in December 1958 when Blossom was summarily fired by a solidly segregationist school board. The crisis dramatized not only the fierce conflict between the segregationist White Citizens' Councils and the integrationist black churches and NAACP but also the determined use of legal and quasi-legal tactics by local, state, and federal authorities in the effort to shape educational policy. In the end, the Little Rock schools were caught between shouting mobs defying federal court rulings and paratroopers brandishing fixed bayonets to enforce those rulings— with the children, as is often the case, in the middle.

The New York City crisis of 1968 was emblematic of the struggle over school decentralization in the nation's inner cities and the conflicts that erupted between militant parents and laypeople on local school boards and organized teachers. In New York the problems in the Ocean Hill–Brownsville experimental school district in Brooklyn were exacerbated by the fact that most of the local school board members and parents were black and most of the teachers involved were white. In a series of bitter confrontations that pitted a local school board determined to run the elementary and middle schools of its district according to its own best lights and a teachers union determined to protect the rights of its members as guaranteed by its contract, the United Federation of Teachers struck the schools of the entire city three times, the last time for five weeks. The crisis dramatized the shifting patterns of political power in those cities where blacks were becoming the dominant clientele of the public school system, where teachers and school administrators remained predominantly white, and where the schools seemed to be failing dismally in the task of educating their students. Once again, the children were caught in the middle.

The Kanawha County, West Virginia, crisis (Kanawha County includes the city of Charleston) epitomized the struggles over fundamentalist versus modernist religious values in the schools during the 1970s and 1980s. It called to mind some of the parent-teacher conflicts of the New York City crisis, though the issues in Kanawha County were religious rather than racial. The controversy erupted during the spring of 1974 when Superintendent of Schools Kenneth V. Underwood asked the school board to adopt several series of textbooks for a language arts program that was to be inaugurated in September. The titles had been chosen by a committee of professionals associated with the Kanawha County schools from an approved state list that had been compiled in accordance with a new state requirement that textbooks for the public schools be "multiethnic." One member of the board, the wife of a local Baptist minister, charged that the books were absolutely unfit for school use, claiming that they undermined the Christian religion, employed "filthy language," featured the writings of convicted criminals, subverted traditional morality, and preached unpatriotic values. The board adopted the books by a vote of 3 to 2, setting the stage for a protracted disruption of the Kanawha County schools that involved boycotts, shootings, firebombings, and dynamitings and that actually closed the schools for a time owing to the superintendent's fears for the safety of the children. The disputed books were then reviewed by a committee of eighteen citizens, which concluded that they were perfectly suitable for school use. In the end, the board stuck by its decision to adopt the books but provided that no child whose parents objected to them would be forced to read them. The community remained deeply divided, and the teaching staff suffered severe demoralization. Yet again, the children were caught in the middle.

The political issues that tore the colleges and universities apart from time to time during the post–World War II era were similarly emblematic of the growing politicization of education. One might cite the conflict at the University of California between 1949 and 1952 over the imposition of a loyalty oath as a condition of employment; the controversies at a score of colleges and universities during the congressional investigations of the 1950s into the political beliefs and associations of professors and administrators; the pitched battles at Columbia, Harvard, Cornell, and other institutions between 1968 and 1971 over student activism associated with the Vietnam War, defense-related university research, and alleged race discrimination; and the somewhat more restrained but no less significant strife at Stanford, Duke, and other universities during the 1980s concerning the nature and substance of the so-called Western civilization requirement for undergraduates.

The same thing was true of the political crises over family and child-care policy—one need only scan the reports of the three regional White House Conferences on the Family in 1980 to grasp the extent to which family policy served as a battleground for conflicts over women's rights, gay rights, abortion rights, family planning, sex education, and child care. And the same thing was true, too, of the political crises over telecommunications policy, where controversies over morality and cultural quality, particularly with respect to children's programming, were not different from those in Kanawha County, with some viewers urging closer regulation by the Federal Communications Commission, others urging boycotts of advertisers who sponsored so-called offensive programs, and still others maintaining that all television broadcasting fell within the guarantees of the First Amendment to the United States Constitution.

II

Thus did education become increasingly politicized during the post-War era, and thus did various groups with differing conceptions of the good life contend with increasing vigor and occasional violence over the nature and character of education. But the question remains, Why? And the answer, I believe, lies in the longstanding American tendency to try to solve social, political, and economic problems through educational means, and in so doing to invest education with all kinds of millennial hopes and expectations. That tendency pushed educative institutions and programs toward an ever more direct relevance to the everyday affairs of ordinary men and women: it directed the attention of the schools to nurturing social, civic, and economic competences in their students; and it directed the attention of the colleges and universities, not only to preparing leaders for the various domains of life, but also to undertaking the kinds of research and service activities that would redound to the advantage of the community, the polity, and the

economy. And in pushing educative institutions and programs toward an ever more direct relevance to everyday
affairs, that tendency ended up casting education as a leading weapon in everything from the fight against race discrimination to the war on poverty to the drive for political
and economic competitiveness.

The philosopher Hannah Arendt commented incisively
on these matters in an essay called "The Crisis in Education" that she published during the spring of 1958. The
crisis in education, she observed, was merely one aspect of
a more general crisis that had overtaken the modern world
"everywhere and in almost every sphere of life." But the
crisis was best observed in America, she thought, because
it assumed its most extreme form there. The reason was
that education played a "different and, politically, incomparably more important role [in America] than in other countries." This was in part because of the historic need to
Americanize the immigrants, she argued. But, even more
important, it derived from the "extraordinary enthusiasm
for the new" in American life and especially for "newcomers by birth," namely, children and young people. Arendt
saw that enthusiasm as a kind of political utopianism, an
illusion that sprang directly from the historic American experience of founding a new nation—a new order of the
ages, or *novus ordo seclorum,* as emblazoned on the Great Seal
of the United States. It was an illusion, she believed, that
could have disastrous consequences in the field of politics.
She cited as an example the federal effort to correct the
intolerable situation with respect to discrimination against
black people in the United States. What did Washington
do? It began with the children in the schools, assuming that
once a miniature model of a just world had been created for
children, it would go on developing naturally and automatically like the children themselves. The plan could not con-

ceivably work, she argued, since the children would eventually grow up into a preexisting world of adults who had been incapable of solving the problem of race discrimination in the first place. And thus, she concluded, did the crisis in education ultimately announce the bankruptcy of progressive education. For Arendt, John Dewey's ideal school as "embryonic community life" could never be the deepest and best guarantee of a larger society that was "worthy, lovely, and harmonious." It could only be a utopian community completely out of touch with reality.[3]

Insofar as Arendt pointed to the limitations upon education's ability radically to change the world, Dewey would doubtless have agreed. One need only review his essays during the 1930s on education and politics in the *Social Frontier* to grasp this fact. Yet despite Arendt's predictions, *Brown v. Board of Education* did bring about social and political change. It brought change, first, through the extension of its principles of equality into other domains, from voting rights to fair employment to fair housing; education was not required to achieve the task of eliminating racial discrimination by itself. Of equal importance, the *Brown* decision brought changes in education that made differences in how children thought, felt, and behaved when they became adults. Jomills Henry Braddock II, Robert Crain, and James McPartland reviewed a good deal of the research literature on the effects of school desegregation in 1984 on the thirtieth anniversary of *Brown* and reported the following findings: (1) black students who had been educated in desegregated elementary and secondary schools were more likely than their counterparts from segregated schools to attend predominantly white colleges and universities; (2) black students who had been educated in desegregated schools were more likely than their counterparts from segregated schools to have white as well as black friends, to live in racially mixed neighborhoods, and to work in racially mixed settings; (3) white and black students who had attended desegregated schools were more likely to have positive attitudes toward future interracial situations than their counterparts from segregated schools; (4) black students who had been educated in desegregated high schools achieved better grades in college than their counterparts who had been educated in segregated high schools, and had higher graduation rates as well; (5) black students from desegregated schools had better employment opportunities than their counterparts from segregated schools, and black graduates of predominantly white colleges and universities enjoyed higher incomes than their counterparts from predominantly black institutions. The authors concluded that "the evidence already in hand tells us that the initial conception of the impact of school desegregation, as expressed in 1954 in the *Brown* decision, has been borne out. The schools are the place in which society socializes its next generation of citizens. The research findings that we have presented here suggest that the U.S. cannot afford segregated schools, if this nation is genuinely committed to providing equality of opportunity to every citizen." My own view would be to modify that statement with the qualification that the socialization of the schools worked to the extent that the schools' efforts to eliminate race discrimination connected with the expansion of desegregation in the community, the polity, and the economy, much of it mandated by government in response to a civil rights movement in which blacks had played a leading role.[4]

What about the role of education as a centerpiece in the War on Poverty during the 1960s? How effective was education in furthering the social, political, and economic goals of that effort? Three acts of Congress were central in the war: the Economic Opportunity Act of 1964, the Elementary and Secondary Education Act of 1965, and the Higher Education Act of 1965. The key educational contributions of the Economic Opportunity Act were Head Start and the job training programs established under the National Youth Corps and the Job Corps. The key educational contributions of the Elementary and Secondary Education Act were the Title I (later Chapter I) programs intended to provide special educational services to disadvantaged children. The key educational contributions of the Higher Education Act were the grants and loans to students attending two- and four-year colleges (they later became the Basic Educational Opportunity Grants under the Higher Education Amendments of 1972). Together these programs were intended, in the words of President Lyndon Johnson, "not only to relieve the symptoms of poverty, but to cure it and, above all, to prevent it." Once again, there were skeptics who called attention to the millennialism implicit in Johnson's hyperbole. Christopher Jencks argued in the spring of 1964, well before the three pieces of legislation had even been enacted, that educational programs were not an effective weapon against poverty, and that the way to eliminate poverty was rather to redistribute income, either directly or by subsidizing the goods and services needed by the poor—an argument he would make again eight years later in the concluding paragraphs of his book *Inequality*. [5]

What actually happened? First, it is clear that the programs did not eliminate poverty. Even if, sufficiently financed and properly conducted, the programs had had that potential, they were increasingly starved of funds by the demands of the Vietnam War and, as a result of inadequate financing, the people who directed them were also deprived of the opportunity to learn from their mistakes. Nevertheless, the programs did make significant differences. In a review undertaken in 1974, Ralph Tyler found (1) that there had been a steady increase in the number of ESEA Title I programs that were providing measurable improvements in the educational achievement of disadvantaged children; (2) that there had been a continuing surge in college enrollments during the late 1960s and early 1970s owing to the high birthrates of the 1950s, the larger percentages of young people graduating from high schools, and the larger percentages of high school graduates going on to college, and that, while the federal assistance made available by the Higher Education Act had clearly made a difference in the participation of black and other minority children in these developments, it was not possible to separate the factors influencing the changes; (3) that early Head Start programs had varied tremendously in their organization and philosophy and that some had clearly begun to produce positive results, but that in light of the considerable reduction in funds during the early 1970s, it was too early to make a general assessment (Tyler had only the results of the 1969 Westinghouse Learning Corporation evaluation to go by, and those results tended to be negative); and (4) that Job Corps programs had demonstrated that many young people from impoverished backgrounds could be helped to acquire the knowledge, skills, and attitudes required for constructive work roles, but that the task was even more difficult and more costly than the original planners had estimated. Tyler's general conclusion was characteristically wise and prudent:

> It is clear now that disadvantaged children can gain in education, but this requires changes in their total educational experiences from early childhood to adolescence. This necessitates large financial support and commitment to long term programs. The returns from these larger expenditures, however, should come not only from the contributions made to this generation of children and youth, but also to those who follow. Disadvantaged children

who gain an education today are educated parents of the next generation. Their children will not suffer the same handicaps that they encountered. But without an adequate program for educating today's disadvantaged, there seems little likelihood that there will be fewer disadvantaged in the next generation. An adequate program reaching the 20 per cent of American children who are disadvantaged and are distributed among thousands of schools requires a long-term commitment to furnish funds and to develop programs under professional competence needed to guide them. An entire generation of children is involved, which means a 20-year effort. The experience of the 1960's suggests that the cost will be two or three times that of educating children of middle-class background. The development of programs and materials and the acquisition of professional competence to guide new programs is likely to take five to eight years. Americans are not accustomed to long-term commitments of this magnitude. It is a real challenge.

As has been pointed out, six years later L. J. Schweinhart and David Weikart, studying the outcomes of the Perry Preschool Program in Ypsilanti, Michigan, found that those enrolled in the program derived long-term benefits from their participation. In later childhood and adolescence they earned higher marks in school and showed greater commitment to schooling, decreased deviant behavior at school, decreased delinquent behavior outside of school, and higher employment rates as teenagers than their peers who had not been enrolled in the program.[6]

Once again, it is important to remember that these results occurred in an educational system and in an economy that continued to expand, however variable the pace of that expansion in different periods and places, and in a polity with legal prohibitions against discrimination in education and employment, however variable the vigor of enforcement in different periods and places. The results of particular educational programs joined with more general changes in the economy and polity to which the results contributed and by which they were confirmed. There were places in the elementary schools for graduates of the Perry Preschool Program; there were places in the high schools for recipients of services under the Title I programs authorized by the Elementary and Secondary Education Act; there were places in the colleges for recipients of the grants and loans made available under the Higher Education Act; and there were jobs—though never enough decent, well-paying jobs that held out hope for advancement—for graduates of the high schools and colleges. In the absence of those conditions, the educational programs of the War on Poverty would have been utopian at best, politically incendiary at worst.

What about the uses of education to achieve political and economic competitiveness? Let us examine two cases: the effort during the 1960s to develop educational and cultural affairs as what Philip Coombs called a "fourth dimension" of foreign policy (the first three being political, economic, and military), and the effort during the 1980s to develop education as an instrument for achieving economic competitiveness—the concern of the sixties being the challenge of the USSR., the concern of the eighties being the challenge of Japan.

It was President John Kennedy who for all intents and purposes launched the first effort. Within weeks after his inauguration, he announced that his administration intended to place greater emphasis on the human side of foreign policy, that there was no better way to assist the emerging nations to become free and viable societies than to help them "develop their human resources through education," and that the best way in general to strengthen the bonds of understanding and friendship with other nations was through educational and cultural exchange. Kennedy envisioned a significant expansion not only of government exchange and assistance programs but also of related efforts by foundations, universities, and other private institutions. To provide a greater measure of coordination and cooperation among various government agencies as well as between the governmental and the private sectors, he announced the creation of a new assistant secretaryship of state for educational and cultural affairs in the State Department and appointed Philip Coombs to the position.[7]

There followed for seven or eight years—again, until the Vietnam War began to consume growing portions of the nation's resources—an ambitious program of technical assistance for economic development that was increasingly cast in educational terms. Scores of American universities received AID contracts to provide expertise in the domains of education, agriculture, public administration, and business administration; the Peace Corps sent thousands of volunteers to conduct schools in the developing nations of Africa and Asia; the Ford, Rockefeller, and Carnegie foundations invested millions of dollars in programs of education, training, and research on the problems of political and economic development, technical assistance, and international education; and the Fulbright and Smith-Mundt exchange fellowships were consolidated and expanded under the Fulbright-Hays Act of 1961, making possible an increased flow of scholars, scientists, artists, athletes, and students between the United States and foreign countries.

There was an undeniable measure of disinterestedness about the effort, as congressional leaders like J. W. Fulbright and Wayne Hays fought unceasingly to separate educational and cultural affairs programs from the government's information and propaganda campaigns and as the sponsors and implementors of the programs in the foundations and universities sought to carry out their educational tasks in a nonpartisan, professional manner. But it was difficult from the outset to separate the educational and cultural sides of foreign policy from the political, economic, and military sides. Furthermore, the educational and cultural sides were given only a fraction of the funds allocated to the political, economic, and military sides, and their power and potency were therefore drastically limited—when a major shift appeared in political relations with the USSR or India or Iran, education was virtually powerless to make a difference. Most important, perhaps, many of the assumptions about the power of education to transform the politics and economics of third-world nations (in the terminology of the sixties, to "modernize" them) proved incorrect at best, dangerous at worse. As anthropologists like Margaret Mead and Sol Tax early pointed out, one cannot simply transplant American educative institutions to foreign cultures without producing massive unintended and unanticipated consequences, some of them exceedingly harmful in the eyes of the host country. Little wonder that twenty years later, the African educator W. Senteza Kajubi would lament the gap between expectation and achievement as he reviewed the educational development of the newly emergent African nations during the 1960s and 1970s:

> In the last two decades a great deal of investment has been made in education with a view to promoting economic and social development in Africa. National governments devote very high proportions of their recurrent and development budgets to education. Organs of the United Nations, friendly governments, and philanthropic organizations have also directed large sums of money and technical assistance toward education with the hope of lessening the economic and social development gap between Africa and the rest of the world.
>
> The green revolutions that were expected from education, however, have not yet occurred. On the contrary, the scenario that Africa presents after two decades of independence is still one of acute and worsening poverty and social and political turmoil. Al-

though commendable achievements have been made in expanding education and health services, universal primary education is far from being achieved in most African countries, and out of every one hundred babies born to African mothers fifteen to twenty die before they see their first birthday. Even among adults, untimely death still strikes hard in Africa. Although Africa has vast virgin arable lands and enormous economic potential awaiting fuller development, abject poverty, malnutrition, kwashiorkor, and starvation are endemic and widespread throughout the continent. In other words, despite the heavy investment in education, Africa remains a problem continent and a disaster area in perpetual crisis.

In the absence of associated political, social, economic, and cultural changes in the host societies, the American educational effort had proved in large measure utopian. It is true that certain of the exchange activities that had gone forward regardless of the state of U.S.-Soviet relations had proved invaluable in advancing mutual interests during periods of relaxation in the Cold War. But even in that instance the educational value of the exchanges was ultimately dependent upon political benefits from the exchanges that appeared to be of mutual interest to both nations.[8]

What about the more recent effort to use education as an instrument to achieve economic competitiveness, particularly with Japan but also with the other booming capitalist economies of eastern and southern Asia? Although few of the data are in, I believe some observations can still be made. To begin, there can be no denying that the skills of literacy and critical thinking that are properly associated with effective school programs are essential to a modern economy and that the schools ought to be held accountable for nurturing those skills in all children. The continued advance of those skills through the entire population will undoubtedly aid the development of the American economy. Nevertheless, American economic competitiveness with Japan and other nations is to a considerable degree a function of monetary, trade, and industrial policy, and of decisions made by the President and Congress, the Federal Reserve Board, and the federal Departments of the Treasury and Commerce and Labor. Therefore, to contend that problems of international competitiveness can be solved by educational reform, especially educational reform defined solely as school reform, is not merely utopian and millennialist, it is at best foolish and at worst a crass effort to direct attention away from those truly responsible for doing something about competitiveness and to lay the burden instead on the schools. It is a device that has been used repeatedly in the history of American education—by the proponents of vocational education in the first years of the twentieth century, when they contended that the Germans were getting ahead of the Americans in industrial efficiency; by the proponents of science education in the 1950s, when they laid the blame for Russia's being first to launch a space satellite on the weaknesses of American schools (not granting, as the quip went at the time, that the Russians' German scientists had simply gotten ahead of the Americans' German scientists); and by the proponents of academicist education in the 1980s as the antidote to the economic threat posed by Japan. The pattern bespeaks a crisis mentality inseparable from the millennial expectations Americans have held of their schools.

III

Let us recall Aristotle's dicta about education and politics. It is impossible to talk about education apart from a conception of the good life; people will inevitably differ in their conceptions of the good life, and hence they will inevitably differ on matters of education; therefore the discussion of education falls squarely within the domain of politics. Steeped as they were in Renaissance culture, early Americans tended to accept these dicta, and indeed some of the most cogent discussions of educational policy in the late eighteenth and early nineteenth centuries were presented in the context of proposals for the political future of the new nation—one thinks immediately of John Adams, Benjamin Rush, Noah Webster, and, towering above them all, Thomas Jefferson. Later, as Americans moved education increasingly to the center of their political affairs, they began to argue the obverse of the Aristotelian dicta as well, namely, that when people differ in their views of education, they are really debating alternative views of the good life, of the kind of America they would prefer to live in and what it might mean to be an American, and that politics is therefore ultimately a branch of education. To recall Dewey's phrasing of the argument: education is the fundamental method of social progress and reform, and all reforms that rest simply upon the enactment of laws or the threatening of penalties or upon changes in mechanical or outward arrangements are, in the end, transitory and futile. For Dewey, education became the means, par excellence, not only for defining the nature of the ideal America and the character of the ideal American but also for bringing both into existence.[9]

Actually, this process of defining what it meant to be an American began well before the Revolution. The initial colonies of European immigrants, predominantly English but also Spanish, Dutch, French, Swedish, and German, were established in a land that had long been populated by a variety of Indian peoples with their own historic civilizations. The Europeans and the Indians lived side by side, trading with one another, occasionally warring upon one another, and inevitably learning from one another. The Europeans established their own configurations of education—households, churches, and occasionally schools and print shops—to ensure the perpetuation of their particular traditions, while the Indians continued to maintain their own ancient forms of nurturance and training. European missionaries did try to Christianize the Indians and in the process to "civilize" them, but there was no large-scale effort to assimilate them to the transplanted European communities—they were widely judged to be unassimilable. Meanwhile, large numbers of African-Americans were brought involuntarily to the colonies, to be sold into slavery. Arriving as individuals or in small family groups, they were attached to the households of Europeans and were forcibly introduced to European languages and European ways. They too were pronounced unassimilable by definition, partly because it was early decided that the slave status of the mother would automatically attach to her children and partly because the racial barrier proved far less penetrable in North America than in South America.

During the seventeenth century, the dominant pattern was one of small, competing ethnoreligious communities, each seeking to reproduce itself through the traditional institutions of education, primarily households and churches. It was in the eighteenth century, however, that a discernible British-American provincial community came into being. Its origins lay in several sources. For one thing, despite the diversity of the seventeenth-century population, the English had predominated from the beginning; and the substantial Scots and Scotch-Irish immigrations of the eighteenth century, coupled with the British victories in the intercolonial wars, went far toward securing the dominance of the English language and of English laws and

institutions. Beyond that, the growing experience of intercolonial cooperation in military, commercial, and religious
affairs after the 1750s did much to create a common American identity. Although individuals still described themselves as Scotsmen or Germans or Pennsylvanians or
New Englanders, they increasingly thought of themselves
as Americans too. Finally, British-American churches,
schools, libraries, and printing presses, supported in substantial measure by British money gathered and disbursed
by the Society for the Propagation of the Gospel in Foreign
Parts, were more numerous and more powerful than those
of other provincial communities, and one result was the
predominance of the English language and culture.

The appearance of an emergent British-American provincial community created for the first time a culture in
which what was American was defined partly in contradis-
tinction to what was not. One sees the phenomenon in the
early eighteenth century when Benjamin Franklin warned
that the British-American community would soon be over-
whelmed by the large German influx into Pennsylvania. It
would become a German colony, Franklin predicted, unless
steps were taken to assimilate the Germans to British-
American ways. It was in light of such fears that Franklin
and a number of his associates set out to establish a system
of charity schools expressly created for the purpose of ab-
sorbing the German immigrants. Not surprisingly, the Germans resisted the effort, and under the leadership of the
printer Christopher Saur, they ultimately defeated it. In
fact, the most important outcome of Franklin's project was
probably in stimulating the Germans to redouble their efforts to perpetuate their own language and culture. In the
end, however, the Germans were assimilated, not instantly
but over several generations, and not through charity
schools deliberately organized for that purpose but

through growing participation in the political, economic, and cultural affairs of the larger American community of which they were part.

All this changed radically with the founding of the republic. The very existence of the new nation implied a fuller definition of nationality, and the very idea of self-government implied a more stringent definition of citizenship. Educational theorists in every quarter proclaimed the need for a new kind of training in knowledge, virtue, and patriotism that would equip the people to perform the duties of citizenship intelligently, responsibly, and with the public interest uppermost in mind. During the course of such argument, a distinctively American *paideia,* or self-conscious culture, emerged. It united the ethos of evangelical Protestantism, the values of the Old and New Testaments, the spirit of *Poor Richard's Almanac,* and the political philosophy of the *Federalist* papers, with the aspirations invoked on the obverse side of the Great Seal by two Latin aphorisms, *Annuit coeptis* ("He [God] has favored our undertakings") and *Novus ordo seclorum* ("A new order of the ages"). The country had its symbols—Brother Jonathan, Uncle Sam, and the Stars and Stripes; it had its patron saints, of whom George Washington was the most illustrious; and it had its popular celebrations, notably the Fourth of July.

Given the emergence of that distinctive *paideia,* the situation for new immigrants changed significantly. Whereas occasional pressure for assimilation had been brought to bear on newcomers during the eighteenth century, relentless pressure for assimilation became the norm during the nineteenth. Moreover, as had been the case with the Germans during the 1750s, the more different the newcomers from the British-American model, the more intense the manifestations of concern. Accordingly, the arrival of large numbers of impoverished Irish and German immigrants during the 1840s, many of them Roman Catholics, evoked heavy pressure for what came to be called Americanization. The Reverend Mr. Lyman Beecher called upon the Protestant churches to save the country from sin in general and popery in particular—by which he meant the Catholic newcomers. Horace Mann called upon the schools to transform immigrant ragamuffins into sturdy young republicans. And Henry J. Raymond used the columns of the *New York Times* to instruct "our adopted citizens" in "the duty of thoroughly Americanizing themselves." The fact that the newcomers did not worship in Beecher's churches, tended to drop out of Mann's schools, and rarely read Raymond's *Times* seemed irrelevant. The native-born Americans who did patronize those institutions heard—and approved—the message.[10]

For the immigrants, the choices were frequently poignant: the dynamics of Americanization were essentially the dynamics of a discordant education. The Irish Catholic families of New York City, crowding into increasingly homogeneous immigrant neighborhoods, maintained their own configurations of Irish households, churches, schools, newspapers, and benevolent societies. New York City, on the other hand, offered public schools, a variety of churches and newspapers, and a dazzling array of social and vocational apprenticeships, most of them unavailable to the Irish. For children and adults alike, the pulls of conflicting loyalties, divergent ambitions, and alternative opportunities were incessant, with the result that the shaping of any particular individual depended upon a complex variety of factors, one of which was invariably luck. Many of the same conflicts were experienced by the Germans who settled in Lancaster, Pennsylvania, although the range of churches, newspapers, and social and vocational opportunities there was infinitesimal in comparison with that of New York, and indeed for a time the German leaders of Lancaster hoped that the county would remain a German enclave within the larger American community. Much the same might also be said for the Norwegian or Swedish Reformed immigrants who settled on the farmlands of Wisconsin and Minnesota and, later, for the Chinese and Japanese immigrants who settled in the cities of California and Washington and the Mexican immigrants who settled in the towns of Texas, Arizona, and New Mexico.

Given the persistence of discordant education through-out the nineteenth and twentieth centuries, several additional points might be made. First, for all the stridency of American nationalism as it developed, the American *paideia* of the nineteenth and early twentieth centuries continued to be loosely and variously defined, with the result that even when immigrants attempted to advance the process of Americanization, as many did, the American society to which they were supposed to be assimilating often proved confusing and elusive. There seemed to be no doubt about the need to learn English, understand the Constitution, and live productively within the law; but beyond that both the models and the principles were frequently unclear. There was much talk after Israel Zangwill's play *The Melting Pot* was produced in 1908 of the merging of diverse nationalities into a new American whole, and there were always people who were ready to define that new American whole with absolute precision, most often along Anglo-American lines. But whether a Jew who spoke perfect English could be an American, or a Roman Catholic who understood the Constitution, or a bilingual Hispanic who lived productively within the law, or a Mormon whose ancestors had come over on the Mayflower, or an Indian whose ancestors had met the Mayflower, remained matters of doubt and controversy. Furthermore, the American culture itself was

constantly being leavened and enriched by immigrant contributions as well as by a steady borrowing of European
(and to a lesser extent, Asian and African) cultural forms so
that immigrants who did contemplate what it might mean
to be an American occasionally saw reflected back upon
themselves some of the very ideas they had expected to
abandon in the process of Americanization.

Second, as successive generations of immigrants came to
the United States, the character of the discordant education
involved in the process of Americanization changed, as the
educative agencies maintained by immigrant communities
for the perpetuation of their own cultures were themselves
transformed by Americanization. More and more, they became agencies not only for the transmission of immigrant
culture to immigrant children but also for the mediation of
American culture to the immigrant community. Thus, by
the 1890s, the Lutheran and Roman Catholic churches
were being torn apart by ecclesiastical and doctrinal controversies over differing attitudes toward accommodation to
American ways; the German Jews of New York City were
supporting educative institutions for the express purpose
of Americanizing the more recently arrived East European
Jews; and the Yiddish press was publishing regular columns
of advice on how to get along in the new country. The
immigrants themselves were not unaware of these developments; and, while some applauded, others withdrew into
orthodoxy, purging their educative institutions of corrupt-
ing American forms and insulating themselves against cor-
rupting American influences.

Finally, the problems of race persisted. Just as African-
Americans and Indians had been defined as unassimilable,
so were immigrants from Asia. The Fourteenth Amendment to the United States Constitution did bestow citizenship upon "all persons born or naturalized in the United

States, and subject to the jurisdiction thereof." But discrimination against African-Americans continued, while Indians
were judged subject to the jurisdiction, not of the United
States, but of their tribal "nations." Even after 1924, when
the Indians were granted full citizenship by special congressional legislation, their status as wards of the federal government left their situation ambiguous. As for the Chinese
and Japanese, the first generations of immigrants were denied naturalization, while their American-born children
were hesitantly accepted as citizens—the deplorable treatment of the Nisei during World War II poignantly documented that hesitancy. It would take the civil rights revolu-
tions of the 1950s and 1960s to shatter the historic
assumption that people might transcend the barriers of
class, religion, and ethnicity to become full-fledged American, but not the barriers of race.[11]

Two profoundly ironic developments of the early twentieth century wrought a fundamental transformation in
what it meant to be an American. First, the same upsurge
of nativism that led Congress in 1907 to create the Dillingham Commission to investigate the problems of immigration (the commission's forty-one-volume report, published
in 1911, purported to document the "inferiority" of the
"new" immigrants) and that later led Congress drastically
to curtail immigration through the Immigration Acts of
1921 and 1924 also set in motion the vast educational campaign known as the "Americanization movement." Under
the leadership of the educator Peter Roberts, the YMCA
began as early as 1908 to conduct a wide range of Americanization activities in scores of cities across the country,
and at the prodding of the Progressive reformer Frances
Kellor and her Committee for Immigrants in America, the
United States Bureau of Education established a Division of
Immigrant Education (financed by funds Kellor raised from

her wealthy friends) in 1914. The United States Chamber of Commerce formed an Immigration Committee during the winter of 1915–16; the National Education Association created a Department of Immigrant Education in 1921; and churches, schools, businesses, and community centers across the country organized comprehensive Americanization programs, including civics courses for immigrant youngsters, literacy classes for immigrant adults, and Americanization Day celebrations for immigrant families. The campaign extended well into the 1920s and in the end seemed to succeed, if for no other reason than that the Immigration Acts of 1921 and 1924 had cut off most of the clientele at the source.

Second, just as the Americanization movement was getting under way, and partly in response to it, a vigorous national debate arose over precisely what it meant to be an American, and therefore what was involved in the process of Americanization. Whereas few voices outside the immigrant community itself had previously been heard questioning the assumption that immigrants needed to abandon their language, culture, and traditions in order to become Americans, a growing number of native-born as well as immigrant intellectuals now rejected that assumption in favor of more pluralistic and multicultural definitions of Americanism. Jane Addams and Ellen Gates Starr organized the Labor Museum at Hull House to dramatize the significance and worth of immigrant traditions to immigrant children. John Dewey and Horace Kallen wrote of the need to redefine Americanism so that it would come to mean not the abandonment of one identity in favor of another but rather the combining or orchestration of diverse identities. And the young writer Randolph Bourne, in a 1916 essay entitled "Trans-national America," sharply attacked both the melting pot definition of Americanism and the Americanization movement that was propagating it, and called instead for a cosmopolitan, international definition that would be in the making rather than already made.[12]

The ironies inherent in a vigorous Americanization effort that coincided, on the one hand, with legislation restricting immigration, and, on the other hand, with the development of a new cultural pluralism very much shaped the ways in which the problems of what it meant to be an American would be defined during and immediately after World War II. The great immigrations seemed to be over after 1924, and Americanization quickly waned as a burning national issue. True, there were small but significant influxes of immigrants during the next two or three decades—of Jews during the 1930s and 1940s, of Hungarians during the 1950s, and of Central and South Americans during the entire period. But as late as 1965 when she issued a second edition of her book *And Keep Your Powder Dry: An Anthropologist Looks at America,* Margaret Mead proclaimed that all Americans, whatever their origins, had become "third generation in character structure," by which she meant that they no longer needed to outdistance their parents because they were representative of other cultures but only because they were out of date.

The leading social concerns of the era centered not on the integration of foreign-born immigrants into the American community but rather on the integration of native-born minorities on some sort of decent and equitable basis. Probably the most popular effort to formulate an American *paideia* in this era appeared in the Swedish economist Gunnar Myrdal's classic study of American race relations, *An American Dilemma: The Negro Problem and Modern Democracy,* where he explicated the complex of "valuations" he called the "American Creed," which he summed up as "liberty, equality, justice, and fair opportunity for everybody." He saw this creed—one might substitute the term *paideia*—as a commonly held pattern of beliefs (variously arranged and variously practiced by different groups and different individuals) that derived from Christianity, the Enlightenment, the English legal tradition, and American constitutionalism, and he argued that it was universally acknowledged (if not adhered to) and served as a prime moving force in American life. He saw the "American dilemma" as the contradiction between the creed that most Americans professed and their failure to afford the most elemental civil and political rights to African-Americans—in Myrdal's words, "The status accorded the Negro in America represents nothing more and nothing less than a century-long lag of public morals." Not surprisingly, Myrdal saw the most important agenda of Americans as one of bringing their practices into conformity with their creed.[13]

For all the incisiveness of the Mead and Myrdal analyses, two large social developments of the postwar era drastically altered the climate of belief with respect to Americanization. The first was the new ethnoreligiosity, the second was the new immigration. Together they not only changed popular definitions of what it meant to be an American, they also revived pressures for a more traditional style of Americanization centered on fluency in English, knowledge of the Constitution and of American civic practice, and the ability to live productively within the law.

The new ethnoreligiosity had several sources. As early as 1955, Will Herberg in *Protestant-Catholic-Jew: An Essay in Religious Sociology* put forward the thesis of America as "triple melting pot," citing in support of his interpretation the aphorism of the late historian Marcus Lee Hansen to the effect that what the second generation wanted to forget, the third generation wanted to remember, or what the children of immigrants wanted to leave behind in an effort to adapt to American ways, the grandchildren of immigrants were attempting to find again in their quest for identity within American society. Downplaying ethnicity in favor of religiosity, Herberg portrayed three great religious communities—equally legitimate, equally American, and equally committed to a common set of moral ideas and spiritual values—as Americanizing communities, each, incidentally, entitled to its own publicly supported schools as instruments of that Americanizing process. Other scholars like Daniel Patrick Moynihan, Nathan Glazer, and Milton Gordon put forward an alternative view that was in many ways the converse of Herberg's, namely, the thesis of America as "multiple melting pot" with a series of transformed and transforming ethnic groups as Americanizing communities. It was but a short analytical leap to combine the analyses and focus on the historic inseparability of particular ethnic groups and the religions they espoused—for example, East-European Jews, Irish Catholics, and African-American Protestants.[14]

A second source for the new ethnoreligiosity was the black-led civil rights movement of the 1950s and 1960s. As ethnic pride—centering on African-American history, African-American studies, and African-American consciousness—mounted in the African-American community, and as an increasingly self-conscious "black power" element began to advance political and social equality for African-Americans, Native Americans, Hispanics, Italians, and Asians followed suit. They began organizing their own legal defense and education organizations, promoting their own ethnic history, ethnic studies, and ethnic consciousness, and mounting their own efforts to advance political and social equality for their adherents. In the process, African-Americans themselves were increasingly transformed into an ethnic group, while a variety of ethnic groups were increasingly transformed into political interest groups. The result was a widespread political, social, and ideological affirmation of ethnicity that transformed the meaning of what it meant to be an American. The influence of pluralism was immeasurably advanced, symbolized best by the development of so-called bilingual-bicultural education programs in the schools as mandated by the United States Supreme Court decision in the case of *Lau v. Nichols* (1974) and authorized by the Education Amendments of 1974, with their provisions for bilingual-bicultural education programs for *all* children of limited English-speaking ability, for "capacity building" grants to aid in the development of teacher training programs, curriculum development, and research activities, and for the development of ethnic heritage study centers.

The new immigration began in the 1950s as large numbers of individuals from the Caribbean, Central and South America, and Canada came to the United States, many as sojourners, others as permanent residents. Those from Puerto Rico were already citizens; those from other countries came illegally as well as legally, moving back and forth across American borders with sufficient ease and in sufficient numbers so that the official figures from the United States Immigration and Naturalization Service conformed less and less to reality. In 1965, the Hart-Celler Act abolished the national origins quota arrangement and the prohibition against nationals of the Asia-Pacific Triangle and provided that applicants were to be admitted on a first-come-first-served basis. The result was a significant rise in the total number of immigrants, legal and illegal, as well as a shift in their origins to include large numbers from south and southeast Asia and the Middle East. The official numbers from the Immigration and Naturalization Service indi-

cated that 4.2 million arrived during the 1970s, but estimates of the actual number ranged from 6 to 10 million,
with most of the illegal newcomers arriving as sojourners
from Mexico and the Caribbean.

When the new immigration combined with the new ethnoreligiosity, the result was, on the one hand, a strengthening of the trend toward pluralism, and, on the other, a
revival of traditional demands for Americanization. In
states like California, Colorado, Arizona, and Florida, En-
glish-only movements arose out of fear of Hispanic separa-
tion and domination. At the national level, opposition to
programs of bilingual-bicultural education intensified—
Secretary of Education William J. Bennett lambasted them
as ill-conceived and ineffectual during his 1984–1988 in-
cumbency. And there were renewed demands for additional emphasis in the schools on the teaching of civics in
general and of American history in particular. Every indica-
tor in the early 1980s pointed toward the beginning of a
new nationwide Americanization movement not unlike the
one that flourished during the second and third decades of
the century, and toward a return to definitions of what it
meant to be an American that closely resembled those of
the earlier era.

The politics of the emerging Americanization controversy, however, was neither as simple nor as predictable as
had earlier been the case. The leader of the California En-
glish-only movement was former senator S. I. Hayakawa, a
Canadian-born American citizen of Asian background; and
the opposition included many native-born white Anglo-
Saxon Protestants. Black ethnic groups in Los Angeles
pressed vigorously for school desegregation throughout
the 1960s, 1970s, and 1980s; Hispanic groups during the
1970s and 1980s preferred segregated schools with effective programs of bilingual-bicultural education. More gen-

erally, the new ethnoreligiosity was sufficiently all-embrac-
ing that one might have every reason to expect division
within as well as among ethnic groups on issues of Americanization. In the end, as Dewey had suggested, a debate
over education was really a debate over the kind of America
people wanted to live in and over what it might mean to be
an American. Politics had indeed become a branch of education.

IV

Education cannot take the place of politics, though it is
inescapably involved in politics, and education is rarely a
sufficient instrument for achieving political goals, though it
is almost always a necessary condition for achieving political goals. Given the demands of the American democratic
system on citizen participation, certain educational tasks
must be performed by child care centers, schools, colleges,
television broadcasters, and other educative institutions if
citizens are to acquire the knowledge, values, skills, and
experience to act intelligently and responsibly on matters
of public concern. Given the demands of the emerging
American economy on workers at all levels, there are certain educational tasks that must be performed by child care
centers, schools, colleges, workplaces, and other educative
institutions if men and women are to acquire the knowledge, values, skills, and experience to contribute effectively
and efficiently to that economy. And given the role the
United States is likely to play in the world of the twenty-first
century, there are certain educational tasks that must be
performed by child care centers, schools, colleges, television broadcasters, workplaces, and other educative institutions if individuals of all ages are to learn to live peacefully

and productively with other peoples who are different culturally, independent politically, and yet interdependent economically. The decisions Americans make on these questions will have everything to do with how America fares internationally during the years ahead, and they will ultimately determine what it means to be an American. Indeed, definitions of what it means to be an American will inevitably depend, as Randolph Bourne suggested more than a half century ago, on the interaction between national America and transnational America.

That said, we know far less than we need to know about how to conduct the educational programs that will be required if we are to proceed with confidence. We face the task in our public schools of educating millions of children—fully a third to a half of the enrollment during the decades ahead—drawn from segments of the population with whom our schools have not done well during the past quarter century—the African-Americans, the Hispanics, and the poor who now constitute the majority of our inner-city populations. And we face that task as the demands of the polity, the economy, and the world-at-large become more advanced, more complex, and more insistent by the day. We face similar demands with respect to education in families, workplaces, and other institutions for adults, including colleges, for which we have an even less dependable body of knowledge. Moreover, we have not yet begun to explore or exploit the potential of telecommunications and computer technology, about which we know least but which we may ultimately need most. Margaret Mead once proposed in an article in the *Harvard Business Review* that we divide all education into primary and secondary phases, with primary education referring to "the stage of education in which all children are taught what they need to know in order to be fully human in the world in which they are growing up—including the basic skills of reading and writing and a basic knowledge of numbers, money, geography, transportation and communication, the law, and the nations of the world," and secondary education referring to "an education that is based on primary education and that can be obtained in any amount and at any period during the individual's whole lifetime." In that paradigm, which is the only paradigm sufficient to the world in which we now live, I believe telecommunications and computer technology will surely be a key element of secondary education.[15]

In all these domains, the role of educational research must be central, and yet our performance in that domain has been anything but reassuring. During the first sixty years of the twentieth century, educational research in the United States went forward in a patchwork quilt of institutions—colleges and universities, state departments of education, the research bureaus of local school systems, laboratory schools, not-for-profit organizations like the Educational Testing Service and the National Education Association, and commercial firms like IBM and the American Book Company. By and large, the effort was poorly supported. There was little communication among the scholars working in these various organizations and hence little replication and criticism of experiments and little cumulation of results; and there was even less communication between the scholars and the practitioners whose work their research was supposed to influence for the better. Furthermore, as my colleague Ellen Condliffe Lagemann has made clear, what started out as a complex of "plural worlds of educational research" at the beginning of the century was rapidly transformed during the second and third decades of the century into a single "mainstream" of research that featured quantification, measurement, and reliance on a narrow range of paradigms drawn almost wholly from contemporary psychology.[16]

With the development of the federal initiatives in education that formed the heart of the New Frontier and Great Society programs of the 1960s, there were major efforts to reform the situation. For one thing, there was a steady rise in federal appropriations for educational research, from $4.5 million in 1960 to $32.8 million in 1965 to $100.8 million in 1970 to $245.0 million in 1972. For another, the National Science Foundation in collaboration with the United States Office of Education and a number of philanthropic foundations sponsored a variety of curriculum development programs conducted by teams of academic specialists and educationists interested in upgrading and modernizing the curriculum of the elementary and secondary schools. In addition, under the leadership of Francis Keppel and Harold Howe II as commissioners of education during the 1960s, the federal government established a number of regional education laboratories committed to large programs of educational research and dissemination in particular sections of the country, as well as a series of more specialized educational research centers dedicated to systematic inquiry into particular problems—for example, the problems of elementary education, educational finance and governance, and the education of the handicapped. In addition, under Title IV of the Elementary and Secondary Education Act of 1965, provision was made for fellowships to assist in the training of educational researchers not only by schools and departments of education but also by departments of sociology, anthropology, economics, psychology, and human development—the effort was patently to broaden the scope of the educational research enterprise. Finally, in 1972, Congress created the National Institute of Education to gather together the federal research efforts and focus them on certain research and development needs such as improving student achievement in the basic educational skills; enhancing the ability of schools to provide equal educational opportunity for individuals of limited English-speaking ability, for women, and for the socially and economically disadvantaged; overcoming problems of finance, productivity, and management in educational institutions; and preparing young people and adults for productive careers.

However high-minded the aspirations of the reformers, they were soon chastened by reality. The so-called new curricula in mathematics, physics, biology, and chemistry developed with NSF, OE, and foundation support proved relatively successful with more able students but relatively unsuccessful with the less able. The regional education laboratories, originally envisioned as educational equivalents of the Brookhaven National Laboratory in physics, proved egregiously uneven in the quality of their personnel, programs, management, productivity, research findings, and dissemination activities. Twenty such laboratories were in operation by September 1966, slightly over a year after President Johnson signed the legislation authorizing their establishment, and, together with the research and development centers, they quickly became a lobbying group for the lion's share of federal R & D funds and have remained so ever since. The research scholars trained under the provisions of Title IV of ESEA came into the academic marketplace during the demographic and financial downturn in the fortunes of schools and departments of education in the 1970s and at precisely the time federal support for educational research began to decline in constant dollars. And the National Institute of Education got off to a shaky start during the Nixon and Ford administrations, peaked during the Carter administration, and was abolished during the second Reagan administration, its functions absorbed into the Office of Educational Research and Improvement.

As is well known, a report from the United States General Accounting Office in 1987 on the research and information-gathering efforts of the United States Department of Education from the early 1970s through the mid-1980s indicated, first, that support for research during that period had decreased more than 70 percent in constant dollars, despite the fact that between 1980 and 1984 the federal investment in education had increased by 38 percent and federal support for research in general by about 4 percent, and, second, that the federal dollars actually spent on educational research were increasingly concentrated on programmatic and institutional support for the laboratories and centers, with a consequent decrease in the funds available to individual scholars and groups of scholars initiating their own research projects. Finally, although one could point to a number of domains in which research under the federal initiative had extended and deepened knowledge in the field of education—domains as varied as the social organization of schools, the cognitive development of children, the individualizing of instruction, the measurement of academic achievement, and the teaching of reading and writing—the traditional gap between researchers and practitioners remained as wide as ever. As William James pointed out almost a century ago, research findings in and of themselves rarely tell practitioners precisely what to do; they serve rather as a resource to be drawn upon as particular situations and circumstances require. Beyond that, it is extremely difficult to create in educational institutions the conditions under which practitioners have the time, the opportunity, the interest, and the encouragement to take hold of tested knowledge, make it their own, and translate it into wisdom about how to carry on their work.[17]

More than ever before in our history, we need systematic, dependable knowledge about teaching and learning in school and nonschool contexts, concerning elementary and advanced subject matter, and with respect to the extraordinary range of racial, religious, and ethnic groups that constitute the American people. We need basic research, applied research, and policy research from a variety of disciplinary and interdisciplinary perspectives; we need to know much more than we now know about how to put the results of that research into the hands of practitioners during their initial training and throughout their careers; and we need to learn how to draw practitioners far more closely into the conduct of that research than we have in the past. In short, we can no longer proceed on the time-honored assumption that some youngsters will inevitably fail in school and that some adults will inevitably remain illiterate and ignorant. Yet we face the stark fact that while the Department of Defense has a research budget that represents some 12 percent of its total budget, the Department of Education has a research budget that represents just under 2 percent of its total budget. Until this situation is changed markedly, it is sheer nonsense to talk about excellence in American education. Ultimately, I believe the sponsorship of educational research on a large-scale and enduring basis must become a prime responsibility of the federal government.[18]

In the end, we must place our education programs on a sufficiently solid basis of tested knowledge so that educational opportunity for all people becomes a genuine opportunity to master the knowledge and skills and to learn the values, attitudes, and sensibilities that will enable them to live happily and productively in the modern world. What is at stake is our vision of the kinds of human beings we would hope Americans to be in the last years of the twentieth and first years of the twenty-first centuries, and of the kinds of education that will help bring those human beings into existence. John Dewey liked to define the aim of education as growth, and when he was asked growth toward what, he liked to reply, growth leading to more growth. That was his way of saying that education is subordinate to no end beyond itself, that the aim of education is not merely to make parents, or citizens, or workers, or indeed to surpass the Russians or the Japanese, but ultimately to make human beings who will live life to the fullest, who will continually add to the quality and meaning of their experience and to their ability to direct that experience, and who will participate actively with their fellow human beings in the building of a good society. To create such an education will be no small task in the years ahead, but there is no more important political contribution to be made to the health and vitality of the American democracy and of the world community of which the United States is part.[19]

NOTES

1. John Dewey, *The School and Society* [1899], in *John Dewey: The Middle Works, 1899–1924,* edited by Jo Ann Boydston (15 vols.; Carbondale: Southern Illinois University Press, 1976–1983), 1:19, 20.

2. David Hulburd, *This Happened in Pasadena* (New York: Macmillan, 1951); and James B. Conant, "The Superintendent Was the Target," *New York Times Book Review,* April 29, 1951, 1, 27.

3. Hannah Arendt, "The Crisis in Education," *Partisan Review* (Fall 1958): 494, 495.

4. Jomills Henry Braddock II, Robert L. Crain, and James M. McPartland, "A Long-Term View of School Desegregation: Some Recent Studies of Graduates as Adults," *Phi Delta Kappan,* 66 (December 1984):259–264. See also the discussion in Christine H. Rossell and Willis D. Hawley, eds., *The Consequences of School Desegregation* (Philadelphia: Temple University Press, 1983). As part of a comprehensive analysis of what social scientists have learned about how much a neighborhood or school's mean socioeconomic status affects a child's

life chances, Christopher Jencks and Susan E. Mayer in a 1989 paper reviewed some but not all of the literature on which the Braddock, Crain, and McPartland article was based ("The Social Consequences of Growing Up in a Poor Neighborhood: A Review," to appear in Michael McGeary and Lawrence Lynn, eds., *Concentrated Urban Poverty in America* [Washington, D.C.: National Academy Press, forthcoming]). In general, Jencks and Mayer concluded that the consequences of school desegregation were less clear and decisive, but they did not take issue directly with the Braddock, Crain, and McPartland findings.

5. Lyndon B. Johnson, "Annual Message to the Congress on the State of the Union, January 8, 1964," in *Public Papers of the President of the United States: Lyndon B. Johnson, 1963–1964*, book I (Washington, D.C.: GPO, 1965), 114; Christopher Jencks, "Johnson vs Poverty," *New Republic*, 150 (March 28, 1964):15–18; and Christopher Jencks et al., *Inequality: A Reassessment of the Effect of Family and Schooling in America* (New York: Basic Books, 1972), 265.

6. Ralph W. Tyler, "The Federal Role in Education," *Public Interest*, no. 34 (Winter 1974):164–187; and L. J. Schweinhart and D. P. Weikart, "Young Children Grow Up: The Effects of the Perry Preschool Program on Youths Through Age Fifteen," *Monographs of the High/Scope Educational Research Foundation*, 1980, no. 7.

7. The Kennedy quotation is given in Philip H. Coombs, *The Fourth Dimension of Foreign Policy: Educational and Cultural Affairs* (New York: Harper & Row, 1964), 2.

8. Sol Tax, "The Education of Underprivileged Peoples in Dependent and Independent Territories," *Journal of Negro Education*, 15 (Summer 1946):336–345; Margaret Mead and Ken Heyman, *World Enough: Rethinking the Future* (Boston: Little, Brown, 1975), 210–211; and W. Senteza Kajubi, "Higher Education and the Dilemma of Nation-Building in Africa: A Retrospective and Prospective View," in Andrew Taylor, ed., *Insights into African Education: The Karl W. Bigelow Memorial Lectures* (New York: Teachers College Press, 1984), 43–44. For a more general series of estimates, see Stephen R. Graubard, ed., "A World to Make: Development in Perspective," *Daedalus*, 117 (Winter 1989).

9. John Dewey, "My Pedagogic Creed" [1897], in *John Dewey: The Early Works, 1882–1898* (5 vols.; Carbondale: Southern Illinois University Press, 1969–1972), 5:93.

10. *New York Times*, June 23, 1854, 40.

11. The Constitution of the United States, Article XIV, in Henry Steele Commager, ed., *Documents of American History* (9th ed.; 2 vols.; New York: Appleton-Century-Crofts, 1973), 1:147.

12. Jane Addams, *Twenty Years at Hull-House* (New York: Macmillan, 1910), 235–236; John Dewey, "Nationalizing Education," in National Education Association, *Addresses and Proceedings*, 1916, 183–189; Horace M. Kallen, *Culture and Democracy in the United States: Studies in the Group Psychology of the American Peoples* (New York: Boni & Liveright, 1924); and Randolph Bourne, "Transnational America" [1916], in *The History of a Literary Radical & Other Papers, with an Introduction by Van Wyck Brooks* (reprint ed.; New York: Russell, 1956), 260–284.

13. Margaret Mead, *And Keep Your Powder Dry: An Anthropologist Looks at America* (2d ed.; New York: Morrow, 1965), 52; and Gunnar Myrdal, *An Ameri-*

can Dilemma: The Negro Problem and Modern Democracy (New York: Harper & Brothers, 1944), xlvi–xlviii, 24.

14. Will Herberg, Protestant-Catholic-Jew: An Essay in American Religious Sociology (Garden City, N. Y.: Doubleday, 1955), chap. 2; M. L. Hansen, The Problem of the Third Generation Immigrant (Rock Island, Ill.: Augustana Historical Society, 1938), 9–10; Nathan Glazer and Daniel Patrick Moynihan, Beyond the Melting Pot: The Negroes, Puerto Ricans, Jews, Italians, and Irish of New York City (Cambridge, Mass.: M.I.T. Press, 1963); Glazer and Moynihan, eds., Ethnicity: Theory and Experience (Cambridge, Mass.: Harvard University Press, 1975); and Milton M. Gordon, Assimilation in American Life: The Role of Race, Religion, and National Origins (New York: Oxford University Press, 1964).

15. Margaret Mead, "Thinking Ahead: Why Is Education Obsolete?" Harvard Business Review, 36 (November–December 1958), 166–167.

16. Lee J. Cronbach and Patrick Suppes, eds., Research for Tomorrow's Schools: Disciplined Inquiry for Education (New York: Macmillan, 1969); Richard A. Dershimer, The Federal Government and Educational R & D (Lexington, Mass.: Lexington Books, 1976), chaps. 1–3; and Ellen Condliffe Lagemann, "The Plural Worlds of Educational Research," History of Education Quarterly, 29 (Summer 1989):184–214.

17. Benjamin DeMott, "The Math Wars," American Scholar, 31 (Spring 1962):296–310; U. S. Congress, House of Representatives, 92d Congress, 2d sess., Committee on Education and Labor, Education Research: Prospects and Priorities, January 1972, 1–6; U.S. General Accounting Office, Education Information: Changes in Funds and Priorities Have Affected Production and Quality, November 1987; and William James, Talks to Teachers on Psychology: And to Students on Some of Life's Ideals (New York: Henry Holt, 1899), chap. 1.

18. U. S. Bureau of the Budget, Budget of the United States Government, Fiscal Year 1989, 6f–58, 6f–53, 6f–68, 6f–67.

19. John Dewey, Democracy and Education [1916], in John Dewey: The Middle Works, 1899–1924, edited by Jo Ann Boydston (15 vols.; Carbondale: Southern Illinois University Press, 1976–1983), 9:82–83, 107.

INDEX

Action for Children's Television, 68

Adams, John, 104

Addams, Jane, 112, 126n12

Alexander, Karl L., 47n20

Americanization, 6, 106–118

Annenberg/Corporation for Public Broadcasting Project, 57

Apprenticeship programs, 76, 82n27

Arendt, Hannah, 85, 93–94, 125n3

Aristotle, 85, 103–104

Ashby, Eric, 45–46, 50n43

Association of American Colleges, 32–34, 49n35

Astin, Alexander W., 48n23

Ayres, Leonard P., 13, 14, 47n15

Babbitt, Irving, 4–5, 46n5

Bailey, Thomas R., 82n27

Beecher, Lyman, 108

Bell, Daniel, 58, 79n6

Bell, Richard Q., 80n9

Bell, Terrel H., 30

Bennett, William J., 32, 49n35, 117

Benton, Deborah Parr, 61–62, 80n11

Bertrand, Olivier, 82n27

Bestor, Arthur, 5, 47n7

Bianchi, Suzanne M., 79n1, 79n4

Bilingual-bicultural education, 116, 117

Blakely, Robert J., 68–69, 70, 81n19

Bloom, Allan, 6, 34, 40, 47n8

Bloom, Benjamin, 62, 74, 80n11, 82n26

Blossom, Virgil, 88–89

Botkin, James, 70

Bourdieu, Pierre, 81n15

Bourne, Randolph, 112–113, 119, 126n12

Boyer, Ernest L., 32–34, 49n34–35, 50n41

Braddock, Jomills Henry II, 94–95, 125n4

Brademas, John, 67

Brogan, D. W., 6, 47n7

Brown v. Board of Education, 88, 94–95

Bryce, Jennifer W., 61, 80n11

Bumpass, Larry L., 79n1

Buttenwieser, Peter L., 75

Caplow, Theodore, 54, 79n3

Carnegie Commission on Higher Education, 20–21, 27–29, 44–46. 48n31

Carnegie Corporation of New York, 67, 68, 100

Carnegie Council on Children, 67
Carnegie Council on Policy Studies
    in Higher Education,
    20–21, 44–46
Carnegie Foundation for the
    Advancement of Teaching,
    27, 32–34, 48n23
Carter, Jimmy (James E.), 67, 70
Chickering, Arthur W., 48n23
Child care, 54–55, 65–68. *See also:*
    Family as educator
Children's Defense Fund, 38,
    49n38, 68, 81n18
Children's Television Workshop,
    57
Church as educator, 55, 110
Clark, Reginald M., 80n10
Clarke, Elizabeth, 63
Clarke-Stewart, Alison, 74, 80n10,
    82n26
Cohen, David K., 21, 47n12,
    48n24, 50n40, 80n9
Cohen, Morris Raphael, 63
Coleman, James S., 10, 47n10, 60,
    79n8
College: historical development,
    1–9; standards, 7–12;
    dropouts, 18–21; Conant
    on, 24–25; 1970's reports,
    27–28; 1980's reports,
    32–34; in early 1980's,
    41–42; current situation,
    43–46; policy
    recommendations, 72–78;
    politicization, 91; and War
    on Poverty, 95–97, 99; and
    international competition,
    99–103; research on,
    120–124
Commission on Higher Education
    (1946), 15–16, 18–19, 45,
    47n18
Committee for Economic
    Development, 32, 49n34
Committee for Immigrants in
    America, 111
Community college. *See* College
Comprehensive Child
    Development Act (1971),
    66–67

Comprehensive Employment and
    Training Act (1973), 76
Conant, James B., 21, 22–25, 33,
    48n26–28, 88, 125n2
Coombs, Philip H., 99–100,
    126n7
Cooper, James Fenimore, 3, 46n3
Cope, Robert, 48n23
Copperman, Paul, 6, 33, 40, 47n8
Corporation for Public
    Broadcasting, 70
Counts, George S., 13–14, 47n16
Crain, Robert L., 94–95, 125n3
Cronbach, Lee J., 127n16
Culture of resistance, 10

Daniels, Denise, 79n8
Day care. *See* Child care
De la Rocha, Olivia, 80n12,
    82n26
DeMott, Benjamin, 127n17
Dershimer, Richard A., 127n16
Desegregation, 94–95
Dewey, John, 7–9, 47n9, 85,
    86–87, 104, 112, 118, 125,
    126n9, 126n12, 127n19
Dillingham Commission, 111
Discordant education, 108–110
Doering, Zahava Blum, 26
Dougherty, Kevin, 47n20
Downey, Thomas J., 68
Dreeben, Robert, 62, 80n12
Dropouts, 12–21
Durham Child Development
    Center, 75
Dworkin, Anthony Gary, 49n37

Eckstein, Max A., 82n27
Ecology of education, viii, 59
Economic Opportunity Act (1964),
    65–66, 95–96
Education Amendments (1974),
    116
Education Commission of the
    States, 32, 49n34
Educational autonomy, 77
Educational Policies Commission,
    15, 47n17
Educational policy: Conant reports,
    22–25; 1970's reports,

Educational policy *(cont.)*
25–29; 1980's reports,
29–34, 39–42, 82n25;
current situation, 42–46;
child care, 65–68;
television, 68–70;
workplace, 70–72; schools
and colleges, 72–78;
post-1945 crises, 87–92;
Arendt on, 93–94;
desegregation, 94–95; War
on Poverty, 95–99;
international competition,
99–103; Americanization,
106–118; educational
research, 120–124
Educational research, 120–124
Educational Testing Service, 71,
120
Educative style, 53
Eisenhower, Dwight D., 89
Ekstrom, Ruth B., 48n22
Elementary and Secondary
Education Act (1965), 39,
95–96, 99, 121
Erikson, Erik H., 60, 79n8
Eurich, Nell P., 58–59, 70–71,
79n7, 81n22

Family as educator, viii, 52–55,
59–64, 91. *See also:* Child
care
Farrar, Eleanor, 50n40, 80n9
Faubus, Orville, 88–89
Federal Communications
Commission, 68, 69, 92
Fine, Michelle, 20, 48n22
Flegenheimer, Arthur (Dutch
Schultz), 63
Flexner, Abraham, 4–5, 46n5
Ford Foundation, 100
Fulbright, J. W., 100–101
Fulbright-Hays Act (1961), 100
Fundamentalists, 9, 90–91

Gallo, Frank, 82n27
Gans, Herbert J., 69, 81n19
Garber, Herbert, 49n39
Gardner, David P., 30
Gardner, Howard, 43

Garet, Michael S., 21, 48n24
General Educational Development
credential, 16, 64, 80n14
GI Bill of Rights, 16
Gifford, Bernard R., 50n40
Glazer, Nathan, 115, 127n14
Goertz, Margaret E., 48n22
Goodlad, John I., 37, 40, 49n37,
49n39, 50n40–41, 74–75,
82n26
Gordon, Milton, 115
Goslin, Willard, 87–88
Graubard, Allen, 25, 48n29
Grosvenor, Gilbert M., 11–12

Hamilton, Stephen F., 82n27
Hannah, William, 48n23
Hansen, Marcus Lee, 114–115,
127n14
Hart-Celler Act (1965), 116–117
Hawley, Willis D., 125n4
Hayakawa, S. I., 117
Hays, Wayne, 100–101
Head Start, 65–66, 68, 96–98
Hefferlin, JB Lon, 48n21
Heffner, Richard, 34–35
Herberg, Will, 114–115, 127n14
Herbert Spencer Education Club,
4
Heyman, Ken, 126n8
Higher Education Act (1965), 96,
99
Higher Education Amendments
(1972), 96, 97
Hildyard, Angela, 81n15
Hoffer, Thomas, 10, 47n10
Holupka, Scott, 47n20
Howe, Harold II, 121
Hulburd, David, 87, 125n2
Husén, Torsten, 50n40
Hutchins, Robert M., 4–6, 7–9,
46n5, 47n9
Hylla, Erich, 5, 46n6

Ianni, Francis A. J., 79n8
Immigrants, 51, 52, 104–118
Immigration Acts (1921, 1924),
111–112
Intelligence, conceptions of,
42–43, 64–65

Jackson, Philip W., 40
James, William, 123, 127n17
Javelgi, Rajshekhar G., 47n20
Jencks, Christopher, 125n4, 126n5
Jefferson, Thomas, 85–86, 104
Job Corps, 96–98
Job Training Partnership Act
    (1982), 76
Johnson, Lyndon B., 96, 122,
    126n5
Junior college. *See* College

Kaestle, Carl F., 71, 82n23
Kahn, Alfred J., 81n18
Kajubi, W. Senteza, 101–102,
    126n8
Kallen, Horace M., 112, 126n12
Kamerman, Sheila B., 81n18
Kanawha County (W. Va.), 87,
    89–90, 92
Katz, Elihu, 60, 79n8
Katz, M. S., 47n16
Kaye, Kenneth, 80n9
Kellor, Frances, 111
Keniston, Kenneth, 60, 67, 79n8,
    81n18
Kennedy, John F., 99–100
Keppel, Francis, 121
Kerr, Clark, 27
Kettering Foundation, 26, 68,
    83n28

Lagemann, Ellen Condliffe, 48n26,
    48n31, 81n15, 120–121,
    127n16
Larsen, Yvonne W., 30
Laski, Harold, 6, 47n7
Lau v. Nichols, 116
Lave, Jean, 62–63, 74, 80n12,
    82n26
Lawrence, Jacob, 64
Learning, 59–65, 74–75
LeCompte, Margaret D., 49n37
Leichter, Hope Jensen, 53, 79n2,
    80n11–12
Levitan, Sar A., 82n27
Library as educator, 26, 77
Liebes, Tamar, 60, 79n8
Life Adjustment Education, 5
Lightfoot, Sara Lawrence, 40, 44,

Lightfoot, Sara Lawrence *(cont.)*
    50n40, 50n42, 62,
    80n12
Literacy, 30, 42, 71
Little Rock (Ark.), 87, 88–89
Livesey, Francis, 4
Lowther, Malcolm A., 75, 82n26
Lynd, Helen Merrell, 54, 79n3
Lynd, Robert S., 54, 79n3

McClintock, Robert, 64, 80n14
McLuhan, Marshall, 51
McPartland, James M., 94–95,
    125n4
Macdonald, Dwight, 35, 49n36
Machlup, Fritz, 58, 79n6
Malizio, Andrew G., 80n14
Mann, Horace, 85, 86, 108
Mares, William, 82n24
Markle Foundation, 68
Mayer, Susan, 125n4
Mead, Margaret, 101, 113, 114,
    119–120, 126n8, 126n13,
    127n15
Melody, William, 68–70, 81n20
Meringoff, Laurene, 62, 80n12
Metz, Mary Haywood, 40, 50n40,
    80n9
Mondale, Walter, 67
Moynihan, Daniel Patrick, 68,
    115, 127n14
Multitudinousness, vii–viii
Murnane, Richard J., 58, 79n7
Murtaugh, Michael, 80n12, 82n26
Museum as educator, 26, 61–62,
    77, 112
Myrdal, Gunnar, 113–114, 126n13

National Academy of Sciences, 32,
    49n34
National Assessment of
    Educational Progress, 71
National Commission on
    Excellence in Education,
    2–3, 6, 21–22, 29–32,
    33–34, 36–37, 39, 46n2,
    47n8, 49n32–33
National Commission on the
    Reform of Secondary
    Education, 25–27, 48n30

National Commission on Testing
    and Public Policy,
    50n40
National Education Association,
    120
National Geographic Society,
    11–12, 47n13
National Institute of Education,
    121–123
National Panel on High School
    and Adolescent Education
    (USOE), 26–27, 30, 48n30
National Science Board, 31–32,
    49n34
National Science Foundation, 18,
    121, 122
National Youth Corps, 96–98
Neill, A. S., 25
Neufeld, Barbara, 47n12
New York City, 87, 89–90
Nixon, Richard M., 66–67
Noah, Harold J., 82n27
Noyelle, Thierry, 82n27

Oakes, Jeannie, 50n40
Office of Educational Research and
    Improvement, 122–123
Ogbu, John U., 10, 47n11
Olson, David R., 81n15
O'Toole, James, 82n24

Packard, Frederick A., 3, 46n3
Pallas, Aaron M., 47n20
Palmer, Edward L., 81n20
Panel on Youth (PSAC), 21,
    25–27, 48n30
Panos, Robert J., 48n23
Parker, Garland G., 47n19
Pasadena (Cal.), 87–88
Passeron, Jean-Claude, 81n15
Pateman, Carole, 82n24
Peace Corps, 100
Perrone, Vito, 40, 50n40, 80n9
Perry Preschool Program
    (Ypsilanti, Mich.), 66,
    98–99
"Pinocchio Effect," 54, 63
Plomin, Robert, 79n8
Politicization, vii, ix, 87–92
Pollack, Judith M., 48n22

Popularization, vii, 1–2, 15–19,
    29, 34–42, 51–52
Powell, Arthur G., 40, 50n40,
    80n9
Professional education, 8, 75
Progressive education, 16–19

Randall, John Herman, Jr., 78
Raymond, Henry J., 108
Resnick, Lauren B., 63, 80n12
Rickover, Hyman G., 5, 47n7
Roberts, Peter, 111
Rock, Donald A., 48n22
Rockefeller Foundation, 100
Roethlisberger, F. J., 80n9
Rossell, Christine H., 125n4
Rowe, David C., 79n8
Rush, Benjamin, 104

Sadler, Michael E., 5, 46n6
Santora, William, 63
Schön, Donald A., 75, 82n26
School: historical development,
    1–7; standards, 7–12;
    dropouts, 12–18; Conant
    on, 22–24; 1970's reports,
    22–24, 26–27; 1980's
    reports, 30–32; political
    dilemmas, 35–38; in early
    1980's, 39–41, 42; current
    situation, 43–45; research
    on, 61–63, 120–124; policy
    recommendations, 72–78;
    politicization, 87–91;
    desegregation, 94–95; and
    War on Poverty, 95–99;
    and international
    competition, 99–103; and
    Americanization, 106,
    108–109, 111–112, 116,
    117
School-based management, 77–78,
    83n28
School Mathematics Study Group,
    18
Schweinhart, L. J., 81n16, 98,
    126n6
Scribner, Sylvia, 74, 82n26
Self-education, 62–65
Seltzer, Vivian Center, 79n8

Servicemen's Readjustment Act
    (1944), 16
Simmons, John, 82n24
Singer, Milton, 81n15
Sizer, Theodore R., 77, 83n28
Smith, Anthony, 79n6
Smith, Marshall S., 39, 49n39
Smith, Sydney, 3–4
Spain, Daphne, 79n1, 79n4
Standards, viii, 2–12, 16–19,
    23–24, 39–42
Stark, Joan S., 75, 82n26
Starr, Ellen Gates, 112
Stedman, Lawrence C., 39, 49n39
Steiner, Gilbert Y., 81n17
Students, 12–21, 38–39, 40, 41,
    61, 75–77, 89–91
Study Group on the State of
    Learning in the Humanities
    in Higher Education
    (NEH), 21, 30, 32–34,
    49n35
Sum, Andrew M., 71, 82n23
Suppes, Patrick, 127n16
Sweet, James A., 79n1
Synagogue as educator, 55

Tax, Sol, 101, 126n8
Teaching, 59–65, 74–75
Television as educator, viii, 53–54,
    55–57, 61–62, 68–70, 77,
    91
Testing, 24, 40, 50n40,
Tinto, Vincent, 21, 47n20, 48n23
Tocqueville, Alexis de, 3–4, 46n3
Toffler, Alvin, 11, 47n12
Torrance, Nancy, 81n15
Trow, Martin, 28, 45, 50n43
Truman, Harry S, 15

Twentieth Century Fund, 31,
    49n34
Tye, Barbara B., 49n39, 50n40
Tye, Kenneth A., 49n37, 50n40
Tyler, Ralph W., 49n39, 96, 98,
    126n6

Underwood, Kenneth V., 90–91
United Federation of Teachers, 90
United States Department of
    Defense, 124
United States Department of
    Education, 123–124
United States General Accounting
    Office, 123, 127n17
United States Office of Education,
    18, 121, 122
University, 23, 28, 45–46, 91
UPS Foundation, 83n28

Valentine, Jeanette, 81n16
Velez, William, 47n20
Venezky, Richard L., 71, 82n23
Vocational education, 8, 24, 27

War on Poverty, 65–66, 95–99
Webster, Noah, 104
Weikart, David P., 66, 81n16, 98,
    126n6
Weiss, Robert M., 46n4
Whitney, Douglas R., 80n14
Workplace as educator, viii,
    57–59, 70–72, 76, 77,
    82n24, 82n27

Zangwill, Israel, 109
Zigler, Edward, 81n16
Zoll, Allen, 88